You Can Be a
Winning Writer

For permission requests, please contact the publisher at:
Mango Publishing Group
2850 Douglas Road, 3rd Floor
Coral Gables, FL 33134 USA
info@mango.bz

For special orders, quantity sales, course adoptions and corporate sales, please email the publisher at sales@mango.bz. For trade and wholesale sales, please contact Ingram Publisher Services at customer.service@ingramcontent.com or +1.800.509.4887.

You Can Be a Winning Writer: The 4 C's Approach of Successful Authors – Craft, Commitment, Community, and Confidence

Library of Congress Cataloging-in-Publication Number: 2018944497.
ISBN: (paperback) 978-1-63353-742-2, (ebook) 978-1-63353-743-9
BISAC category code: LAN002000 — LANGUAGE ARTS & DISCIPLINES / Authorship

Printed in the United States of America

For all the dreaming writers of the world
and for Adam, my rock.

Contents

Foreword

As I sat reading Joan Gelfand's *You Can Be a Winning Writer* in preparation for writing this foreword, I decided that I needed to stop and get on with writing it. But fascinated, I couldn't. Instead, I found myself nodding *yes, yes, yes* at every paragraph, and often stopping to jot down especially meaningful lines to share with the women and sometimes men in the Zona Rosa Writing and Living Workshops I've led for thirty-seven years.

In this book, Gelfand beautifully and concisely addresses the four seemingly contradictory parts of every successful writer's life: Craft, Commitment, Community and Confidence—the first two we hone in solitude, our butt in a chair or our nose in book after book; the second two when we put ourselves out into the world to join forces with our literary peers and heroes (who, as she mentions, sometime become friends and supporters). Over and over, she nails the myth of the solitary artist, and rarely has an author described so succinctly what we need as writers—from initial inspiration to the long haul of publication.

As I read, memories of my own early years as a writer flooded through me, and I realized afresh how fortunate I had been to have had all four of Gelfand's requirements on my side. As a mother of three, a woman afflicted with post-partum depression, and a high school dropout who had never heard of Emily Dickinson or T.S. Eliot, after I took a class in Modern Poetry at Emory University and the professor read work from great modern poets, I was evangelized in a way I never had been in the Bible Belt Baptist Church I'd grown up in. Next, I took a poetry workshop, and while my kids were in nursery school each day, I wrote and rewrote the poems that had begun pouring out of me and copied poems I loved into notebooks, analyzing how their authors had written them. Craft and Commitment by then became my obsession.

Shortly after, my teacher—a grad student destined to become a well-known poet himself—invited me to join a writing workshop. The workshop ended up being made of Emory professors and their wives—PhDs who laughed when I could neither pronounce nor spell Nietzsche, enunciated *Oedipus Rex* as "O-ped-ius Rex," and when I explained why I'd put an "ejaculation" point at the end of each line. Nevertheless, they supported my work, providing Community and Confidence. Indeed, I was the perfect example of Samuel Clemens' (a.k.a., Mark Twain's) words, "With ignorance and confidence, success is certain."

Thereafter, and many times during my decades as a writer, Gelfand's Four C's for being a winning writer have played themselves out in my life. For example, when I bought my first manual typewriter (on time, and yes, it was that many years ago!) and a typewriter table, and then, twelve years later, when I rented a room away from home in which to finish my first collection of poems (Craft and Commitment again). "If you're good enough, you'll be published," my first editor Jennifer said to me, inspiring me to work harder.

Several years later, published in both memoir and fiction, I gave myself over to the excitement and pleasure of promoting my second, third, and other books on book tours. The same book tours that put me—after years spent in solitude at my desk—on national television and at large literary venues, calling again on the need for Community and Confidence. While reading *You Can Be a Winning Writer*, I realized afresh what a large part—and how constantly, as though in a rhythmic dance—Gelfand's Four C's have played in my writing life. (And a special note: Gelfand, like me, was a poet first. And she, like me, recommends writing and/or reading poetry—the most concise literary form—to every writer, whatever his or her chosen genre may be.)

Dense with great examples, bountiful in its outpouring of concrete advice, and full of the joy of being part of a special tribe, *You Can Be a Winning Writer* is the book I wish I had when I first fell in love with the art of writing. It is a book in which every writer will find the help and inspiration they need—wherever they may be on their writing journey—and I will recommend it time and time again.

Rosemary Daniell

ROSEMARY DANIELL is the founder and leader of Zona Rosa, a series of writing workshops attended by thousands of women, and some men, with events in Atlanta, Savannah, and other cities, as well as in Europe, which has been featured in *People* and *Southern Living*. She is also the award-winning author of nine books of poetry and prose, including *Secrets of the Zona Rosa: How Writing (and Sisterhood) Can Change Women's Lives* and *The Woman Who Spilled Words All Over Herself: Writing and Living the Zona Rosa Way*, and is the recipient of two National Endowment for the Arts fellowships in writing, poetry, and fiction. Rosemary's work has been featured in many magazines and papers, including *Harper's Bazaar, New York Woman, Travel & Leisure, The New York Times Book Review, Newsday, The Chicago Tribune, The Philadelphia Inquirer* and *Mother Jones*. She has also been a guest on many national radio and television shows, such as *The Merve Griffin Show, Donahue, The Diane Rehm Show, Larry King Live* and CNN's "Portrait of America." Early in her career, she instigated and led writing workshops in women's prisons in Georgia and Wyoming, served as program director for Georgia's Poetry in the Schools program, and worked for a dozen years in Poetry in the Schools programs in Georgia, South Carolina, and Wyoming. In 2008, she received a Governor's Award in the Humanities for her impact on the state of Georgia. She is profiled in the book *Feminists Who Changed America, 1963–1975*. For further information, write Rosemary at rosemary@myzonarosa.com.

Tribe

By Rosemary Daniell

A poem written after the Associated Writers Conference in Tampa, Florida, 2018.

We meet on 13th Street

in this city we're not familiar with—

poets, novelists, memoirists, academics.

"So good to see you," we say again and again

the air thick with ego, desire, aspiration

thousands upon thousands of us

the weird ones who spend—some would say, waste—

our lives putting words, ideas, truths in order.

Like cat or butterflies filling a vast field

we radiate, connect with joy

already thinking of next year in Portland—

sure for once of our purpose

and at last, with our own kind.

A Letter from the Author

"Nothing stinks like a pile of unpublished writing."

—Sylvia Plath

Mastering the Four C's of Successful Writers: Craft, Commitment, Community, and Confidence

If you have ever suffered the sting of rejection, this book is for you. If you have started a book, but haven't finished it (though God knows you've tried!), this book is for you. If you have sent out a manuscript which you labored over, believe in, and want to see in print with a burning passion, but haven't found a publisher, this book is for you.

If you have been told that your work is not marketable, if you have felt isolated, frustrated, and confused, *You Can Be a Winning Writer* is here to help. In this book, I'll teach you how to tease apart the obstacles that hold you back. In these chapters, you will find support, anecdotes, and inspirational quotes that will encourage you to confront, face, and overcome your most challenging issues. You'll find encouragement to finish that first book, find a publisher, and sell books.

College/Shaw
Toronto Public Library
College/Shaw 416-393-7668

User ID: 27131042692360

Title: You can be a winning
writer : the 4 C's approach
Item ID: 37131201713377
Date due: 08 December 2018
23:59

Telephone Renewal 416-395-
5505
www.torontopubliclibrary.ca

I wrote this book for writers who have never seen the inside of a university. I wrote the book for MFA graduates who have crafted a great piece of writing, but are not yet on the path to publication. I wrote the book for writers who have waited years until retirement to write the novel or memoir that's been haunting them, and for mid-life writers who have decided to tell their secrets, or their most fantastical story.

I wrote *You Can Be a Winning Writer* for poets who aspire to write their first novel, for journalists struggling to find the time to write a full-length investigative book, for history buffs intrigued by mysterious figures from the past. I wrote the book for any writer who dreams of seeing their work in the hands of a multitude of readers.

The Four C's approach was a system I devised that brought me across the chasm from aspiring writer to published author. The approach also helped me to win a list of awards and nominations I had never dreamed of.

When I told a friend about this book, he asked what advice I could possibly offer writers that hadn't already been written.

"There are books on craft. There are books on 'the business of writing.' But I have yet to see a book that incorporates all the building blocks: commitment, community-building, and confidence as integral to becoming a winning writer," I told him.

In the past few years, books on building a platform, constructing compelling plotlines, and making good scripts great have flooded the market. Books on screenwriting, playwriting, the craft of the novel, and television writing advise writers on how to get their books written in a timely and

YOU CAN BE A WINNING WRITER

successful manner. I'm a fan of many of these books, and, in the resources section, I provide a list of recommended reading.

You Can Be a Winning Writer might very well be the only holistic approach to becoming not just a writer with a publishing credit, but a writer who relishes success.

What do I mean by holistic? Holistic is defined as "incorporating the concept of 'holism' or the idea that the whole is more than merely the sum of its parts, in theory or practice."

By incorporating the four key aspects of the writing life, *You Can Be a Winning Writer* provides practical and real-world instructions on becoming a successful author.

With discussions by experts, published authors, and successful writers on the thrills, the challenges, and the vicissitudes of the writing life, I believe that this book will inspire you to aspire to greater heights, to think bigger and to reach for the brass rings of your dreams.

I've lectured on how to be a winning writer for over ten years at literary festivals, writer's conferences and universities. And I've coached writers individually to great success.

The goal of *You Can Be a Winning Writer* is to eliminate the drama, the emotional slowdowns, and the self-doubt that hinders and keeps you, all the talented authors, from publishing success.

Joan Gelfand

June 2018

Introduction

Mastering the Four C's

Early in my career, after some moderate success as a poet, I got bitten by "novel fever." Post-college, I had had a fair number of poems published in literary journals. I had performed at prestigious venues like the Oakland Museum, Litquake and the Beat Museum. I had even had the excellent fortune to have a poem turned into a song and recorded by a rock band. The song was aired on the local radio station and nationally. But I still didn't feel like a winning writer.

I didn't set out to write a novel. I mean, really? I had cut my teeth on Simone de Beauvoir, Virginia Woolf, Willa Cather, Kurt Vonnegut, Gunter Grass, and Wallace Stegner. I was satisfied being a poet, known to my local community.

Writing a novel seemed like a terribly pretentious, misguided idea. No. I did not start out to write a novel. I started out with a story that, after two years, and much encouragement from my writing instructor, grew into three hundred pages. I had written my first novel without planning to do so.

It was with that first novel that I began to understand that becoming a successful writer wasn't just about writing. It was several years after my first attempt to find a publisher for that first novel that I understood the business of writing.

I learned that the letter I got back from an agent asking me to revise my manuscript was a serious request, not a rejection. And, I learned the hard way that without confidence, without commitment and community, I was never going to become a winning writer.

Understanding the Four C's

While the Four C's approach encourages you to improve your craft, it also provides suggestions for the design of a productive work practice, recommends ways to cultivate a supportive network, and gives clear and practical examples of how to build your confidence. What makes the Four C's approach unique is that I will teach you how to develop all these skills at the same time.

Does it sound like a lot of work? It is.

Over the years, I've coached innumerable writers who start out insisting that they barely have time for the actual writing. Just getting to their desks, crafting a piece of writing, and finishing it is a tremendous challenge. And it is. But just finishing a piece of writing is not enough.

After just a few sessions of working with me, these same writers find their priorities shifting as they begin to understand the importance of cultivating a network and building community. They realize that sending out their work one or even ten times is not enough. Soon, they find themselves more confident about every aspect of their work.

I've worked with clients who, after secretly aspiring to see their work in journals that publish their "writing heroes," find themselves side by side those very same heroes.

I've worked with professionals who do not consider themselves writers, but manage to get the help they need to tell their story and get their important books into the hands of the public.

The Four C's system: Imagine that your writing career is a stove with four burners.

Craft. Commitment. Community. Confidence.

Each burner has a pot on it that needs to be watched. Each pot is cooking up something tasty.

Craft is bubbling while commitment is on a low simmer; you are out in the community, seen everywhere! That pot is on full boil. While you were out, confidence has scalded; that last manuscript rejection has you wondering if you've got what it takes. Who said you could write your way out of a paper bag anyway?

As the Head Chef de Cuisine, your job is to fire up all burners at the same time. Your job is to attend to them to make sure one is not boiling over while the others are stalled.

Juggling is involved. Timing is essential. But this is your *piece de resistance*! You can do it.

What Are the Four C's?

On the front burners are craft and commitment. On the back burners are community and confidence.

Whether you are a seasoned cook, or have never donned an apron, whether you are Cordon Bleu trained or a self-starter who learned to steam fish from a YouTube video, you are about to create this special meal. Winning writers keep all burners warm.

It is not an easy task. It's demanding. It requires an exacting sense of timing, keeping a keen eye on the clock and the intuition to adjust the seasoning just right. It might also require a last-minute replacement of a burned dish, a broken plate, or repairing a malfunctioning burner.

Why work so hard?

Your project at hand is a book, right? You're not really preparing a meal for twenty. Or are you?

Let me explain: In the past, writers, many of whom self-identified as "introverts" could sell a manuscript to a reputable publishing house. The editor and the house believed in them, supported them as a member of that house's family. The publisher assigned a publicist and a marketing budget. New books were added onto a publisher's list which book reps reviewed with book buyers when they visited bookstores. In the past, the marketing department kicked into gear, and, if everything went according to plan, the book was well reviewed. Voila! Book sold. Self-identified introverted author didn't have to go on book tour if he/she didn't want to. If all went well, that author could have a shot at another book. If the book didn't sell, it was remaindered.

Fast forward to 2018. On the one hand, publishing is in a sea change and on the other hand publishing is the same as it ever was. Did you know that Walt Whitman self-published *Leaves of Grass*? Walt Whitman! Jack Canfield and Mark Victor Hansen self-published *Chicken Soup for the Soul*. Other best sellers that were self-published include *Fifty Shades of Grey*, *What Color is Your Parachute?*, and a long list of iconic books.

With a healthy dose of the Four C's, all became bestsellers.

Part of the sea change is that writers can no longer afford the luxury of living the life of an introvert. The writer's life has become a cruel paradox; the work that requires a person to possess high thresholds of tolerance for solitude now requires high thresholds for public speaking, promotion, and public appearances!

Talk about anxiety-producing! So how does a private person become a winning writer? With patience, a custom menu plan and determination, most writers can follow the Four C's of successful authors.

And here's the good news. Mastering the Four C's becomes easier over time. Once the four pots are simmering away, readers catch a whiff of your excellent cooking! Now there's a crowd congregating around the stove. Murmurs of "Mmm..." and, "How did she do that?" start to hum. A buzz is going around about this "chef" who appears to be everywhere! Readers are curious!

Now, you can turn down the flame on one burner and turn up another. But not one step can be overlooked or ignored when you are getting started. All your skills will be tested. All your perseverance will be tried. Your confidence will be challenged.

You will want to quit. There's a reason the saying goes, "If you can't stand the heat, get out of the kitchen."

Backstory

In the chapters that follow, you will learn how to refine your craft. You will learn how to manage the first dozen—or hundred!—rejections. You'll learn how to build your reputation as you are writing your book. You'll learn how to build your fan base even before your book hits the stands. And when that book comes out, you'll learn how to speak to your fans, making each one feel important and loved.

The long and winding road:

A few years out of graduate school, I received what every writer dreams about: a love letter from a top agent: "You are clearly very talented. Your book is compelling, but the second half falls down. Please let us know what you decide to do."

I had hired a writer's assistant to send my first novel to agents. I didn't realize that this agent who had praised my work and was asking me to take a closer look at the second half was the agent of the Pulitzer Prize-winning author Michael Chabon.

This is what we writers call "the backstory." Established authors can't help but chuckle when an author is touted as an overnight success; we know the years it took to hone the craft and get the project out into the world. Even Steph Curry didn't make the cut for the NBA in his early years.

Each author has a unique backstory. While mine is particularly circuitous, you'll see from the anecdotes peppered throughout this book, I have lots of company.

When the dream letter arrived, I was working full-time and raising a child on my own. I owned a home and was caring for an aging mother. I was writing from 5:30 a.m. to 8:00 a.m. before I dropped my sleepy, pajama-clad toddler to daycare and got myself to work.

I had just met the man who was to become my husband. His response to the encouraging missive from the New York agent was that the letter was an open door, a chance, and a golden opportunity: "Quit your job and write!" The edict came with an offer to help me financially. He didn't have to ask twice. "I'll have this book published in a year," I promised. He already knew what a hard worker I was. He saw how focused and determined I could be. As Adam Gopnik, a columnist for the *New Yorker*, writes: "No one is hungrier than a writer staking out his reputation." At the time, I was in corporate sales and had been a top producer in my field for over ten years.

Unschooled in the Four C's at the time and naïve about the pitfalls of the literary world, innocent about the vicissitudes and the complex maze of getting books published, I took my book to an editor I had read about in the professional press.

I didn't take the time to vet her or research her reputation with writers. Her advertisement proclaimed that she was a Pulitzer Prize-winning novelist and editor. From where I sat, I would be lucky to get her attention.

"Your female characters are male, and your male characters are female." Ouch. And, in not so many words, she proclaimed the book was no good. She even pulled a book off her shelf to compare a passage I had written about loss to a published novel. Cowed, I was sure my book was a loser. The letter from the New York agent must not have meant anything. The agent must just have been feeling generous and decided to be kind to an aspiring novelist.

How easy it is to diminish praise.

"Many writers learn to write by writing their first book," said the Pulitzer Prize-winning editor. "What else do you want to write about?"

At that time, I actually was anxious to start a book about the characters I had come to know in the tech world. I agreed to put the novel that I'd spent the previous five years writing on the shelf.

Starting a new book meant that I wouldn't have to confront these terrible flaws that this charming editor had brought to my attention. Starting a new book meant I could start fresh.

I had a BA and an MFA in Creative Writing. I had been encouraged to write the book I was about to shelve by my first writing teacher, a novelist herself, who believed the story, the characters, and the writing to be strong and compelling.

The Pulitzer Prize-winning author billed me a whopping $3,500 and washed her hands of me. I never even got a write-up of comments. Her work was a wholesale smash job.

How quickly I put five years of writing, revising, and editing on the shelf, not to mention the years of getting up at 5:00 a.m. to write for two hours before work. Unbeknownst to me, the "editor" had a terrible reputation for tearing writers down.

What happens next is that I blew it. Big time.

Chapter 1

Craft

Crafting a Great Piece of Writing

"Anyone who is an inspired storyteller...knows that the essence of good storytelling is not assembling a heap of facts but having the imagination to leap through an arc of bright truths to create a great arc of invention. A story is a constellation of stars, a recognizable shape made from shining bits of fact that may exist empirically at different levels and different spatial depth."

—Adam Gopnik, on the author Romain Gary, *The New Yorker*, January 2018

While Gopnik describes writing, he himself crafts an impressive piece of journalistic prose. By using imagery (an arc of bright truths), analogy (a story is a constellation of stars), and metaphor (the story exists empirically at different levels and different spatial depths), Gopnik crafts a sentence that you want to read over and over. You might like to contemplate "a constellation of stars" or how a story exists at different levels and different spatial depths.

By using basic tools of craft, he creates a memorable paragraph, as well as an excellent argument.

When I taught poetry to school-aged children, we broke down teaching into five basic elements:

- Imagery—draw a picture with words.

- Sound—use words to clash, rhyme and accentuate each other.

- Repetition—use the same words to make your piece memorable and incantational.

- Analogy and metaphor.

- By using the five senses—sight, hearing, taste, smell, and touch—your writing will come alive with the specifics of the world.

It is common knowledge that many poets have become novelists of extraordinary success.

Michael Ondaatje and Alice Walker are just two examples. Because poetry is a kind of shorthand, an unforgiving and compact form (no wasteful words, no unsubstantiated arguments or theses), writers who start as poets quickly learn the beauty of the economy of words. Other writers who wrote poetry and fiction were Jorge Luis Borges, Agatha Christie, and Kingsley Amis.

About writer Reed Farrel Coleman: "Poetry was RFC's first calling, and it also brought him to crime fiction: 'I heard the poetry in the language of Chandler and Hammett, listened to the meter behind their words, and thought that I wanted to try my hand at it,' he writes on his website. 'The truth is, I knew I could do it. I realized, at last, that all those poetry writing classes and the classes I'd taken in Renaissance, Romantic,

Victorian, and modern poetry had been more than fascinating wastes of my time.' "[1]

"A book has to smell. You have to hold it in your hand and breathe it in."

—Ray Bradbury

So how long should your book be? Two hundred pages? Three hundred? Seven hundred? How much is enough, and how much is too much? On the importance of the economy of language, novelist Ethan Canin taught: "Could you write in three words what you just wrote in ten?"

This teaching could not be of more importance now. Now that we receive a virtual tidal wave of information, readers read quickly; they want to get the point, and get it fast.

Oh, and what we also taught children? Don't be afraid of humor!

And, always let your imagination run loose. Have fun. (Remember Dr. Seuss? Whimsical, nonsensical, and so beloved!)

Poet Stephen Kopel, San Francisco writer, radio host, and organizer of the Word Dancer literary series, sees himself as a thorough craftsperson in shaping stacks of words into

---

1   Reprinted from *LitHub Daily*, 2018.

YOU CAN BE A WINNING WRITER

something beautiful, thoughtful, comical and pleasurable to both readers and listeners.

Kopel begins with concept. "My journey into the world of language...is fraught with possibilities...thank goodness. My principal interest is having as much fun in both concept and composition as I can muster toward that end. I first start with a composition of lines in which associative values, a dose of punnery, and the breaking apart of multisyllabic nouns can be expanded into two or more words."

For the reader's continued pleasure, here is an example of two lines from "Prankster" by Stephen Kopel:

```
                    "the
                    Wind"

    please put on a summer show, a carnival of
                   shrieks,
              skinny sounds or fat.
```

Adam Gopnik, above, spoke of a story as existing "at different levels and different spatial depths."

Poet Mary Mackey, author of fourteen novels and seven volumes of poetry, and the winner of the Josephine Miles award from PEN, taught creative writing at Sacramento State University for over thirty years. She calls it "layering," but it is the same concept. By using language creatively, you can take a reader from one level of experience to another in just a few words.

"Purity"
By Billy Collins

My favorite time to write is in the late
afternoon,
weekdays, particularly Wednesdays.
This is how I get about it:
I take a fresh pot of tea into my study and
close the door.
Then I remove my clothes and leave them in a
pile
as if I had melted to death and my legacy
consisted of only
a white shirt, a pair of pants and a pot of
cold tea.

Then I remove my flesh and hang it over a
chair.
I slide it off my bones like a silken
garment.
I do this so that what I write will be pure,
completely rinsed of the carnal,
uncontaminated by the preoccupations of the
body.

Finally I remove each of my organs and
arrange them
on a small table near the window.
I do not want to hear their ancient rhythms
when I am trying to tap out my own drumbeat.

Now I sit down at the desk, ready to begin.
I am entirely pure: nothing but a skeleton
at a typewriter.

Take the line "as if I had melted to
death and my legacy consisted only/of a

> white shirt, a pair of pants and a pot of
> cold tea."

The words melted to death bring us from the world of a poet sitting at his desk, to an imaginary world, a world of fantasy and dream.

"I remove my flesh and hang it over a chair." Now we are in the place of poetry. We are in that multidimensional space where the poet has left his physical surroundings to enter the world of creativity.

This poem is an excellent example of the use of imagination, metaphor and imagery that makes this beloved poem memorable.

From poet and author Mary Mackey:

> "A great poem expands beyond the obvious,
> transcending logic and time, reaching into
> the lyrical, metaphorical depths of language
> and binding together the conscious and
> unconscious. It doesn't just state an idea.
> It exists in multilayered realms, unique,
> ever expanding in the mind of the reader.
> To create these layers, you need to write
> a first draft and then enrich it by making
> sure each line moves in a seamless rhythm
> and each word has powerful associations.
> Don't settle for the first thing that comes
> out of your head. Revise. Revise. There are
> probably twenty better words for 'walk,' not
> all of them synonyms. Don't have your 'rough

> beast, its hour come around at last,' walk
> towards Bethlehem. Have it 'slouch.'"

"Writing is not just words on a page," Tom Parker, Pulitzer Prize nominee for the novel *Anna, Ann, Annie* and author of *Small Business,* advises. Parker echoes Gopnik: "Writing is not just assembling a heap of facts."

At the same time, for many of us, our first drafts are just that. Words on a page. A heap of facts. It is an important part of your writing process and one which we will discuss later in this chapter under the heading "You Wrote It. Now, Revise."

Writing that important first draft without prejudging, without the "critical voice," is how we get started. I can say with confidence that not one author ever published a first draft. I'll bet even Adam Gopnik drafted his stellar piece on writing at least several times as well.

Mary Hayes, author of nine novels—including the *Time* and *Life* bestseller *Amethyst*, her latest novel *What She Had to Do,* and two political thrillers co-authored with Senator Barbara Boxer—says: "We write to discover who we are."

I became a writer because there seemed nothing else I could do.

I'd supported myself, since age seventeen, with a string of unrelated jobs (librarian, fashion model, medical tech) in various countries, knowing a little about a lot but expert in nothing, with no degree or qualification. By thirty-three, as a mother of two young children, I decided to get serious and find a career I could be passionate about. By process of elimination, the professions and sciences seemed closed to me (such long, expensive training to be a doctor, lawyer, or astrophysicist, and could I be passionate *enough?*), and I was too old to launch myself into the arts—except, perhaps, as a writer.

I'd grown up in a bohemian British family of writers and artists, so it was in my genes. I'd always enjoyed telling stories. Writing was cheap; all I needed was paper and a typewriter. So, for three mornings a week, during the two hours when my three-year old was at nursery school and the baby took a nap, I'd ruthlessly churn out at least 2,500 words, butt glued to my seat, no interruptions allowed. I told all my friends about my book so they'd ask how it was going and I'd be forced to finish it out of pride.

It wasn't published (although it would be later), but I didn't give up. I couldn't; by then I'd developed such a strong work habit I'd be restless and anxious if I wasn't at my desk between 10 a.m. and noon.

So, I tried again, and after twenty-two letters of *thanks but not for us,* somebody actually made an offer for my second novel. It was a small paperback house, the money wasn't great, but I was on my way and I've never stopped. I don't believe I can now.

While getting down your first draft, don't fret about whether you are creating a great piece of writing. The first draft is the time to dive into your theses, your character development, your plot. It's in your subsequent drafts that you fine-tune.

Tom Parker again: "First you build the house. Then you screw down the boards."

Many authors express surprise (and delight) at how their characters instruct *them*; tell the writer how to write their lines. Many writers report that their characters dictate their words and actions.

Being open to all kinds of surprises when you sit down to write is part of being a winning writer. You might have the plot down cold, but a twist might unfold as you are writing—go for it.

It is exactly this element of surprise that will delight your reader. As Pulitzer Prize-winning poet and author of *Walking Light*, Stephen Dunn, writes: "If the writer is not surprised by the ending of a poem, they haven't done their job."

In *Walking Light*, Dunn's collection of essays on writing, he addresses the importance of surprise, especially when writing on political topics:

> "To complain, protest, register outrage, are familiar impulses in most of our lives. And what occurs in our lives inevitably is reflected in poetry. Yet Robert Frost wrote that 'grievances are a form of impatience,' and went on to say that he didn't like them in poetry…. Yeats told us that quarrels with others produce rhetoric."

Later, in the chapter on "Complaint, Complicity, Outrage, and Composition," Dunn targets exactly what causes rhetorical or dogmatic poems to fall flat. After analyzing several successful and unsuccessful poems in the vein of "complaint," Dunn writes: "In any of these poems we could speculate on the varieties of inspiration which spurred them, though, I think, it's safe to say that the linguistic discoveries in the

YOU CAN BE A WINNING WRITER

act of composition were at least as inspiring as the events or attitudes which preceded them."

To rephrase, Dunn is teaching that you can write a successful poem of complaint or outrage if you allow it to unfold, as any other good writing does. If you allow the poem to lead you, to surprise you. "Locate a poem's first real discovery, and often you will find its motor, if not its ignition key."

Writing stories and novels is a different process, yet the basic elements are similar. In all forms of creative writing, "something has to change."

In a novel, it is your protagonist's change that keeps your reader turning the pages. The "big reveal" is the element of your story that you might subtly hint at for the first section. What skeleton does your character hide in his closet?

Another key element to keep your story moving is timing. The minute your book opens, the clock is ticking. As we will read later, *Tinkers*, a first novel that won the Pulitzer Prize, is all about clocks ticking!

Narration: Who's Talking?

Crafting a winning book is the art of crafting a reliable narrator. Is the person telling the story consistent? Are they likable? Trustworthy? Snarky might be trendy, but think about whether you want to read an entire book sustained by a snarky narrator.

Other issues to consider on narration are point of view—first person or omniscient narrator. Would you like to create intimacy with your reader, or keep a cool distance? Italo Calvino, in *If On A Winter's Night A Traveler*, has what is called a "close voice." You feel he is in the room with you, speaking directly to you. That is a writer with an "intimate" voice. On the other hand, Charlotte Bronte, in *Jane Eyre*, maintains a cool distance.

Jonathan Franzen on narrative voices and gaining the reader's trust:

> "Every writer is first a member of a community of readers, and the deepest purpose of reading and writing fiction is to sustain a sense of connectedness, to resist existential loneliness; and so, a novel deserves a reader's attention only as long as the author sustains the reader's trust."

In the classic book *Novel Voices*, edited by Jennifer Levasseur and Kevin Rabelais, the Pulitzer Prize-winning author Richard Ford talks about writing in first person. The interviewer inquires whether Ford feels more comfortable writing in first person, and Ford responds: "I have a much harder time finding redemptive language for events and characters if I am not writing in first person." The stories written (in third person or by an omniscient narrator) "are harsher. The moral quotient to those stories tends to be a more negative kind. They tend to be stories that indict their characters more than the first-person stories. Why? I don't know. But I'd like it to not be so."

In the same book, Ann Patchett talks about how *The Patron Saint of Liars* is told by three first-person narrators. Patchett explains: "I spent a year putting that book together before I started writing it." And, "The last two things I do when I start a book are naming the characters and figuring out the narrative structure. Those are the hardest things for me, and so I put them off as long as possible."

There are many ways to start. Many ways to tell a story. Map it in advance or simply start writing. You will find your way, the way that opens the doors to page after page. The way that allows you to empathize with and understand your characters. There is no one right way.

Construction

Umberto Eco, author of *Name of the Rose*, told an interviewer about his practice of building the architecture of his books. He would not begin writing until all the plot elements were in place, the character's quirks and personalities fully developed.

Like Tom Parker, he also compared writing to building: "First, the foundation, then the framework. You design the rooms and the lighting. Then you decorate."

Like many other writers, the Beat poet and novelist Jack Kerouac wrote his iconic *On the Road* in one long sweep. So did Pearl Buck, who won the Pulitzer Prize for *The Good Earth*.

Trust

Trust is the first part of growing confident in your work. You may have heard the adage: "Trust the process." What exactly does that mean?

The writer Joan Didion addressed the topic of trust in the wonderful Netflix documentary *The Center Will Not Hold*. When asked to speak about her writing process by her nephew (the producer and director of the documentary), Didion replied: "When I sit down to write, the work unfolds."

Didion, a prolific writer who published two novels, a seminal memoir, and countless articles and screenplays, maintained a daily eccentric practice. She would wake up, drink a Coke, eat a few almonds, and set to work.

All writers begin with the germ of an idea. A plot. Characters. But it is only when you sit down to actually flesh out that plot or character do the ideas flower into a beautiful, mysterious garden, fit for a long, leisurely visit.

Be ready for your words to flow. Be open to your own new ideas.

Michael Jackson, the musician, lyricist and creative artist, said "I am just the channel."

The source of your work might be hard research. It might be a mystery. Whichever it is, making the work readable still remains a process and that process is art.

Winning writers are ready for the flowering, to be the channel, and to discover who they are through their work.

As a keynote speaker once pronounced: "Always remember that you writers are in the entertainment business." Employing surprise, delight, bringing your reader to new worlds, fantasy, imagination, and incorporation of the five senses will bring your writing from first draft to winning writing!

> *"Writing a book is like crossing a stream. Now I'm on this rock. Now I'm on this rock."*
>
> —Ann Beattie

Onward!

Practice: Daily or Flow?

New Yorker columnist, pop psychologist and bestselling author Malcolm Gladwell wrote *Outliers*, a book that proves the thesis that it requires "10,000 hours to master a skill." The phrase went viral. Thinkers, musicians, artists, and writers who read Gladwell's book agreed. Here is an excerpt from an article that Gladwell wrote when his theory came under fire:

"Forty years ago, in a paper in *American Scientist*, Herbert Simon and William Chase drew one of the most famous conclusions in the study of expertise:

There are no instant experts in chess—certainly no instant masters or grandmasters. There appears not to be on record any case (including Bobby Fischer)

where a person reached grandmaster level
with less than about a decade's intense
preoccupation with the game. We would
estimate, very roughly, that a master has
spent perhaps 10,000 to 50,000 hours staring
at chess positions...

In the years that followed, an entire
field within psychology grew up devoted
to elaborating on Simon and Chase's
observation—and researchers, time and again,
reached the same conclusion: it takes
a lot of practice to be good at complex
tasks. After Simon and Chase's paper, for
example, the psychologist John Hayes looked
at seventy-six famous classical composers
and found that, in almost every case, those
composers did not create their greatest
work until they had been composing for at
least ten years. (The sole exceptions:
Shostakovich and Paganini, who took nine
years, and Erik Satie, who took eight.)

This is the scholarly tradition I was
referring to in my book *Outliers*, when I
wrote about the 'ten-thousand-hour rule.'
No one succeeds at a high level without
innate talent, I wrote: 'achievement is
talent plus preparation.' But the ten-
thousand-hour research reminds us that
'the closer psychologists look at the
careers of the gifted, the smaller the role
innate talent seems to play and the bigger
the role preparation seems to play.' In
cognitively demanding fields, there are no
naturals. Nobody walks into an operating
room, straight out of a surgical rotation,

> and does world-class neurosurgery. And
> second—and more crucially for the theme of
> *Outliers*—the amount of practice necessary
> for exceptional performance is so extensive
> that people who end up on top need help.
> They invariably have access to lucky breaks
> or privileges or conditions that make
> all those years of practice possible. As
> examples, I focused on the countless hours
> the Beatles spent playing strip clubs in
> Hamburg and the privileged, early access
> Bill Gates and Bill Joy got to computers in
> the nineteen-seventies. 'He has talent by
> the truckload,' I wrote of Joy. 'But that's
> not the only consideration. It never is.' "

I bring this issue up in the interest of becoming a winning writer. An agent friend of mine once said, after I told him that I was revising my novel for a fourth time, "That's good. Very good. The most common problem I see is writers letting go of their work too soon. Work on it until you are satisfied."

In the interest of the craft of writing, a good question to ask yourself is: Are you ready to log those 10,000 hours? How will you do it? Do you like to write in long spurts, working an idea until exhaustion? Or do you prefer to work an hour, or two or four, every day?

What's the trick?

I've read countless articles about how many writers trick themselves into writing. Why? Because the idea of writing for three to five hours a day is intimidating. That the writers don't have the confidence that the words will be there. That, as Joan Didion insists, they don't trust the process. There's a reason that "writer's block" is a topic of endless discussion among students and professionals in the writing world.

Tricks are fine. Whatever gets you to the page.

One trick writers employ is a timer. They set a timer for ten, fifteen or twenty minutes. The rationale is that they can certainly write for twenty minutes! Then, when the timer buzzes, if the work is flowing, off they go!

Recently, the writer Janet Malcolm published a book titled *Forty-One False Starts: Essays on Writers and Artists*. Her fascinating and lengthy essay on the infamous Bloomsbury group gives us the backstory on how a disparate group of intellectuals and artists became ubiquitous in the literary world. Have you ever wondered how an author as experimental, as language-driven and as dreamy as Virginia Woolf became embedded into every college English curriculum? How Bloomsbury captured the imagination of virtually every aspiring author?

"Every day for five to six days a week, they went to their rooms after breakfast. They wrote from 9:30 a.m. until lunchtime at 1:00 p.m. Three and a half hours per day, five to six days per week, 330 days a year. That is why their output was prodigious—novels, memoirs, essays, a prodigious output. In the afternoons and evenings, they walked, they read, they had long discussions," Malcolm writes.

Not every writer has the luxury of time, or the confidence to arrange their lives as the Bloomsbury group did. But what about using a timer to accomplish a minimum of twenty minutes or even an hour per day? Don't forget: hours add up.

Do the math: You write 1,000 words in an hour, that's four pages. Four pages over a month (twenty days) equals eighty pages. Eighty pages over three months equals 240 pages. Congratulations! You just wrote the first draft of your next book!

If you were to research the backstory of now-famous writers, you would learn that a significant percentage wrote their first books on stolen time, in short spurts, on weekends. Toni Morrison wrote in taxicabs while she was working as an editor. Christopher Gortner, author of eight novels, wrote his first three while he was working full-time.

What Are You Afraid Of? A Frank Discussion of Writer's Block and Fear

The fear of writing is real. For many, the idea of a blank page is one of, if not the most, terrifying task. Given any other task—mopping the floor, running a load of laundry, cooking, cleaning the cat box, walking the dog—anything is more appealing than facing that page.

No matter that once the body is in the chair, the words, most of the time, will begin to flow. Still, the fear is, "What if they don't?"

Fear is powerful. We avoid fear in all sorts of ways. We fear planes; we don't buy a ticket. We fear meeting new people; we don't go out to events where we don't know anyone. Our subconscious avoids fear as a survival tool!

Avoiding fear, or any other uncomfortable situation, is called staying in your "comfort zone." Choosing to write will certainly take you out of your comfort zone.

So, before you become a winning writer, you will have to make peace with fear. I'm not a psychologist, but my colleague Renate Stendhal is. We'll hear from her later in our chapter on "Confidence."

Anne Lamott wrote: "I used to not be able to write if there was a dirty dish in the sink. Now I can write if there is a dead body!"

Again, your writing is a practice. Do you work in a rush or methodically?

Joan Didion worked every day, to much success. So did the Bloomsbury group. Many writers believe in a daily writing practice like the pope believes in Jesus.

But how about this for an idea? A "crash"?

Nobel Prize-winning British writer Kazuo Ishiguro wrote *The Remains of the Day* in four weeks. He writes: "Many people work long hours. When it comes to the writing of novels, however, the consensus seems to be that after four hours or so of continuous writing, diminishing returns set in. I'd always more or less gone along with this view, but as the summer of 1987 approached I became convinced that a drastic approach was needed. Lorna, my wife, agreed.... So Lorna and I came up with a plan. I would, for a four-week period, ruthlessly clear my diary and go on what we mysteriously called a "crash." During the crash, I would do nothing but write from 9:00 a.m. through 10:30 p.m., Monday through Saturday. I'd get one hour off for lunch and two for dinner. I'd not see, let alone answer, any mail, and would not go near the phone. No one would come to the house. Lorna, despite her busy schedule, would for this period do my share of the cooking and housework. In this way, so we hoped, I'd not only complete more work quantitatively, but reach a mental state in which my fictional world was more real to me than the actual one…. Throughout the Crash, I wrote free-hand, not caring about the style or if something I wrote in the afternoon contradicted something I'd established in the story that morning. Awful sentences, hideous dialogue, scenes that went nowhere—I let them remain and plowed on."

So, winning writers' styles vary. Daily practice, crash, and "flow." There is no right way.

The movie *Trumbo* tells the story of Dalton Trumbo, the author of Academy Award-winning screenplays and prize-winning novels. Trumbo worked in a fever of alcohol and pills—turning out play after play. His output, like the Bloomsbury group's, was prodigious.

Your style might even vary from project to project. Some poems "write themselves." Others need ten revisions. And some books come very easily. Be open to how your project is going.

Where Did That Come From? A Note on the Source of Writing

I've had students ask, "How can I multiply my ideas for stories, poems, or even my next novel?" A good practice is training yourself to pay close attention. Dorothy Bryant advised: "It is common that while you are working on one project, your creativity is at a fever pitch. You have ideas for other projects. Rather than stop what you are doing, take your notes, file them away. That way you know you've captured the ideas, but they must wait until you finish the project at hand."

For example: You might overhear a couple arguing in a restaurant. A friend might have a gem of insight, but she is not a writer. Ask if you can use her idea—promising proper attribution, of course. Or, you walk into a pet store and two turtles are mating. You're fascinated, so you observe, wait to see if the scene provokes a feeling. You go to a rally, an art show, a movie. It moves you deeply. Try to locate the feelings. That's your germ.

Another approach is to turn your dreams into poetry, prose, songs or any other creative endeavor.

Writer and teacher Sandy Boucher said, "Everyone wants to *have* written." To that, I would like to add "Everyone *dreams* of being a writer."

I'm here to tell—you don't have to dream about it—you can actually use your dreams to source your creativity.

Many famous artists from John Lennon and Paul McCartney to Albert Einstein to Mick Jagger and James Cameron have used their dreams as a source of their creativity.

In Kelly Sullivan Walden's book, *I Had the Strangest Dream*, the author offers tips on remembering your dreams.

1. Sleep with a notebook by your bed—if/when you wake up with a dream, jot down snippets if that's all you have.

2. Incubate a dream: Ask for a dream before you go to sleep.

3. Once the dream is recorded, spend time with it. Look up the images in a dream book and think about the symbols.

Here's a dream from one of Kelly's books:

> A woman is in a bar and another woman approaches her with a drink. As the woman gets close to her, she throws the drink in her face, hits her over the head with a glass, and yells in her face, "Wake up."
>
> And the woman wakes up from her dream and she's covered in water and she's got a bump on her head and she's holding a glass. And she realizes that she did this to herself. She poured water on herself, hit herself on the head and was yelling the words "wake up."

And she sat on the edge of her bed drenched and aching and saying, "What am I supposed to be waking up to?"

She sat down to write. She started journaling and she realized she was journaling for the first time in years. What came through her journaling was, "You're a creative. You have a master's in creative writing and you teach creative writing in schools. You are constantly encouraging your students to write, and yet you have not written creatively in years. You must write."

So, she continued her journaling and it turned into pages and pages and pages of a story, of a fictional story that turned into poetry. Cut to present time. She's changed her life. She's no longer teaching, she's writing full-time and making a living at it. And she's living in Mexico and traveling. She's got a totally different life—unrecognizable from the life that she had at that time.

And some of the background of what was happening at that time in her life was that she had put all of the money that she had made and saved into this "dream house" that was completely falling apart and causing so much stress. And she ends this story by saying, "Instead of plunking all my money down into my dream house, I thought I would just put my money and energy into living my dreams instead."

Recently, my friend Yvonne had a dream about numbers. She tried to remember them in the dream but she couldn't. When she woke up she realized that the numbers were her old address and that she needed to write about a friend who had co-owned the house with her and had died of AIDS.

The story of how I wrote "The Ferlinghetti School of Poetics" is not so unusual, but it did require me to pay attention, to record my dreams and to meditate on them. The poem went on to win an award from the City of San Francisco, and was made into a short film that has been shown around the world.

In the first dream, Lawrence Ferlinghetti made an appearance. That was it. I woke up and said, "Hey, that's cool, I had a dream about a famous poet."

The second dream came some time later—maybe two or three months. In the dream, I am on a dark street instructing a small boy: "You gotta go to the Ferlinghetti School. It's totally rad and completely cool." I'm beginning to think something interesting is happening. Recurring dreams always deserve attention!

In the third dream, Ferlinghetti arrives in a movie theater. By this time, I was thinking "I don't know what it is with Ferlinghetti, but I'm getting a pretty strong message."

But what should I do with it?

I began to craft a poem. I didn't know I had a winner until the poem was published six subsequent times, three times by request.

Sometime after the poem was out and published, I was co-hosting a program on how artists use their dreams with dream expert Kelly Sullivan Walden. I read the Ferlinghetti poem on air. Kelly's husband, musician and filmmaker Dana Walden, fell in love with the poem and asked if I was interested in making a movie of the poem.

Over the next six months we filmed in San Francisco, Los Angeles and Santa Cruz. We spent another few months editing. A year later, we launched the film at the Beat Museum in San Francisco to great reviews.

That little five-minute film went on to be shown at the International Poetry Festival in Athens, Greece, the Meraki Film Festival in Madrid, and numerous venues in San Francisco. The poem won Best Poem of the year from *Levure Litt*éraire, a French literary journal, and the film went viral too, garnering over 12,000 hits on YouTube.

That seemingly innocuous practice of recording my dreams delivered me an award-winning poem and helped me on my way to becoming a winning writer.

I believe that using dreams for art is especially powerful because dreams are "messages" or information from our unconscious, the part of our brains that is most sensitive. The unconscious knows us better than we know ourselves and can tell us what we really feel, even when we are thinking differently.

This is Carl Jung on dreams:

The dream is often occupied with apparently very silly details, thus producing an impression of absurdity, or else it is on the surface so unintelligible as to leave us thoroughly bewildered.

Hence, we always have to overcome a certain resistance before we can seriously set about disentangling the intricate web through patient work.

But when at last we penetrate to its real meaning, we find ourselves deep in the dreamer's secrets and discover with astonishment that an apparently quite senseless dream is in the highest degree significant, and that in reality it speaks only of important and serious matters.

This discovery compels rather more respect for the so-called superstition that dreams have a meaning, to which the rationalistic temper of our age has hitherto given short shrift.

So, go ahead! Capture that gem of an idea and see what evolves.

Writing Workshops, Writing Circles, & Write-a-thons

Even after settling into your writing style (daily practice or flow), you might still be wondering—*How do I get those 10,000 hours/240 pages/poetry manuscript?* Maybe you have tried a daily writing practice, but your words are not adding up. Your kids or full-time job disrupts your best intentions. Sickness, travel, family problems. The list of obstacles that can, and do, derail writers writing practices is long. They are part of life.

Okay. You tried. You failed. The self-flagellation begins.

I can't stick to anything. I'll never be a winning writer. I'm a loser. A failure. Why did I ever think that I could be a writer anyway? Who am I fooling?

These castigations are normal, and unfortunately seem to be part and parcel of the writer's journey. But don't give up hope—not yet!

Here is another idea.

Structured writing environments have set many on the path to winning writers.

In cities, workshops abound. Groups and classes can be found in local community colleges, adult learning centers, private teachers, and writing centers.

Workshop formats vary. One might be a group of writers who meet every week, or every two weeks or once a month. Some workshops employ a formal leader, a professional writing teacher. Others are peer-led.

If you are not in a metropolitan area or even a small town that offers opportunities to meet up with other writers, then you may want to investigate online writing workshops. In the back of this book is a reference list of some of the best online groups.

The advantage of an online group is that many online writing workshop teachers and facilitators run their classes with Skype or Facetime so writers have a chance to have a rigorous experience.

Some workshops require writers to submit work to the group prior to the meetings, while others read the work for the first time at the meeting.

Personal chemistry will impact your experience of the workshop. Do you like your fellow writers and trust them enough to read, and ultimately judge, your work? Do you like their work? Are you working at a similar level of expertise?

The good news:

A well-run workshop, especially for writers just starting out, can be substantially supportive and inspiring. The chance to hear new voices and a wide range of writing styles can help a new writer ascertain where their work falls on the scale of accomplishment.

It can also help to get those pages finished. Knowing that, every second Wednesday (or every Saturday, or Thursday), you will be required to read pages can help to motivate even the most procrastinating of writers. If you like your fellow workshop participants, even more so. Now you are part of a group. You want to show them what you can do, and you go home inspired to write by your fellow writers who are moving along at a steady clip.

However, workshops can be frightening if you've never shared your work in public. To that end, you might want to interview the instructor, sit in on a class or check reviews of the teachers.

Many independently run workshops require an application. The instructor might inquire into your background and goals. Also they will ask to see at least ten to twenty pages of your recent work. If this is the case, then you can safely assume that the level of writing will be above average.

Workshops that do not require an application will be open to writers at all levels. In these classes, you could very well be joined with degreed writers, prize winners, published writers and newbies.

A lively writing workshop can provide a stimulating environment as well as a networking opportunity. Fraternizing with others who are pursuing their dream of writing can help you feel part of a community. And, of course, a good writing instructor can provide just the encouragement you need to keep going. Because if you are working on a long project, doubt will rear its ugly head.

I would never have written my first novel if my gentle and compassionate teacher, Sandy Boucher, had not encouraged me to "just keep going." I went to her workshop with a sketch of a story that she could see as a book-length piece. I just kept going as she advised, and in two years I had a novel. Left to my own devices, I would never have had the confidence to declare myself fit to write a novel!

Here is a beautiful example of a writer nurturing other writers along the path by creating a conscious support group:

Every writer benefits from the promise and support of a writing community. A feedback forum helps cultivate self-editing mastery, deepen craft, and provide confidence to follow through with the next draft. I created the Writer's Tribe to offer up a space for writers to give and receive feedback in the spirit of generosity. In community, we polish our manuscripts in a safe, highly interactive space built on respect, clarity, and honesty. We support and guide each other through a powerful revision process. Writers learn from the comments, notes, and editing suggestions from their fellow participants. These invaluable critiques of our works-in-progress provide a road map and help the group form bonds for the writing process through to the book launch. I've been honored to shepherd new writers who are unable to quiet their inner critics and are afraid to read their work aloud into a community of powerful, successful and confident authors.

Tips on How to Give Feedback

- In the manuscript margins, make comments and suggestions.

- Identify the writer's strengths, interesting subject matter, pleasing shape of the text, and examples of vivid detail.

- During the discussion, read a sentence or craft element you love.

Tips on How to Receive Feedback

- Take every suggestion IN with receptivity and a deep breath.

- Do not defend the text.

- What you resist may be what you most need to hear.

- Ask yourself if the reader's comments are irrelevant or destructive to your process.

- All feedback is golden.

With a writing teacher and the support of writing communities, many students have been launched onto the path of publishing and confidence.

The point is, it is not easy, this "starting out" process.

Jonathan Franzen muses: "When I was writing my first book, I hated going to parties. No matter what the reason for the party, the topic would invariably turn to:

'What do you do?'

'I'm a writer,' I would say.

'Oh? What have you published?'

'Nothing.' "

To avoid this socially awkward encounter, many writers work in stealth mode! They don't tell anyone what they are working on, nor do they mention that they are writing. It's a personal decision to be sure!

The Bad News about Workshops

The bad news is that many independently run workshops should be advertised with warning label: "This workshop may be harmful to your self-esteem."

I had an experience with an editor that set me back in a big way.

I was revising my first novel when I began to feel adrift. I'd left my corporate job based on a note from a NY agent: "You are clearly very talented. This book is compelling and interesting. The second half falls down. Please let us know what you decide to do."

"I'll have this book finished in a few months," I promised myself. But after a few months of revising, I wasn't confident that I was on the right track. At that time, I saw an ad for a pricey writing workshop. I would have dismissed it, but the leaders were a well-known New York editor and a Pulitzer Prize-winning novelist.

Writers were invited to apply. I spoke with the editor, sent in pages, and was allowed to join.

I was not only hoping to get the direction I needed to fix my novel for the New York agent, but secretly hoping to make a connection to people in the literary world.

The workshop, run in a chilly meeting room of Fort Mason, the large warehouse complex in San Francisco waterfront, was filled with accomplished writers; journalists from big-name newspapers and MFA grads.

The critiquing style of the Pulitzer Prize-winning novelist/ teacher was brutal. "God doesn't even care about that goat as much as you do," she chastised one of my fellow writers.

Another bad workshop story, albeit with a happy ending, is the story of Lolly Winston. Winston, the author of the *New York Times* bestselling novel *Good Grief*, had been a student of my teacher Tom Parker. The workshop (comprised of a different group than the one I was in) ridiculed her novel about a young widow. Lolly, to her credit, absented herself from the workshop and finished her novel. She sold the novel which climbed to the *NYT* bestseller list. Soon after publication, *Good Grief* was optioned by none other than Julia Roberts for a movie.

The Lolly Winston story exemplifies the hazards of writing workshops: mind-numbingly harsh feedback, overly critical members and unsupportive groups.

A good rule of thumb before enrolling in any independent writing workshop might be to ask these questions:

Who is teaching? What are his/her credentials?

How do their former students rate them?

What have their students gone on to accomplish?

Remember, in an independent workshop (as opposed to an accredited college class) teachers have not been vetted by strict administrations, do not adhere to a formal pedagogy, and cannot be relied upon to be the teacher that you need.

Barbara Kingsolver cautions to focus on your own voice and finding how best to express it to your own satisfaction first:

"Don't try to figure out what other people want to hear from you; figure out what you have to say. It's the one and only thing you have to offer."

Writing Circles

Often peer-run, critique groups can also be a positive motivator to produce work. When you know that you will be presenting to the group, in some magical way, the pages get written. Writing circles are a lovely and low-key way to use peer pressure to motivate your writing process.

Jackie Berger is the author of four acclaimed books of poetry, three of which have won prestigious awards. She reports:

> "I always tell my graduate students that the best aspect of the program (ours leads to an MA in English with a focus on creative writing) is the community of writers they join. The degree takes two years to earn, but if they can create an ongoing writing group from among their classmates, that will serve them well beyond graduation.
>
> That's what I did. Actually, it took just one woman in my MFA program to invite me to join her group. Twenty-three years later, I'm still meeting with these writers twice a month. They've seen me through four books of poetry, and I can say quite sincerely that I wouldn't be the writer I am without them. By this I mean that they provide a concrete audience for my poetry. They also provide a deadline, the value of which should never be

underestimated! Every other Wednesday night,
I need a new poem. Yes, I'm too busy, too
uninspired, too overwhelmed by life. And I
need a new poem. My writing group gives me
critical feedback, of course, but also a
home for my writing practice—a place to take
it. And this is invaluable.

Solitude is not the same as isolation. We
write alone, but we don't need to go it
alone. And, in fact, much of my raw material
is generated in a group setting as well. In
addition to my Wed. group, I'm in a monthly
Saturday group devoted to freewriting. We
spend an hour or so eating, catching up,
reading to each other authors we love. Then
we each find a room in the house we meet
in to write for an hour or two. After, we
return and read to each other. No critiques;
just reflecting back. I love a pressure
cooker, and nothing like that actual
audience on the other side of the wall to up
the ante.

This is, of course, my process. And what
works for me might not work for you. But
the point is, writers need community, in
whatever form, to tell us that what we have
to say matters. That someone's listening."

Write-a-thons

A "Write-a-thon" is a time set aside to write with a group. A
full Saturday. A weekend. Any time where the writer can give
him or herself a stretch of uninterrupted time. The success

rate is high. Think of it as locking yourself in a room, but with the pleasure of knowing that other people are doing it too.

Have you ever heard of NaNoWriMo? It's National Novel Writing Month, and the idea is a fun, seat-of-your-pants approach to creative writing.

On November 1, participants begin working toward the goal of writing a 50,000-word novel by 11:59 p.m. on November 30.

Valuing enthusiasm, determination, and a deadline, NaNoWriMo is for anyone who has ever thought about writing a novel.

I've heard of writers drafting their novel during NaNoWriMo. Think of it as a version of Ishiguro's Crash. It can be done.

Many writers will also dedicate valuable free time—and money—to attending writer's conferences. Despite the time and expense, most attendees report that the jolt they get from the workshops and talks and being around other writers can be just what they need to get over that next hurdle or challenge.

From *Writer* magazine:

Writer Jennifer Mattson shares her top ten must-go-to conferences for writers, taking conference size, geographical locations, topics and experience levels into account. No matter your background, your interests or your budget, there's a conference on this list for you.

1. The Muse and the Marketplace

Grub Street, a writing center in Boston, holds its annual conference at the Boston Park Plaza Hotel for three days each spring. The weekend draws over 140 well-known authors, literary agents, editors and publishers. (Disclaimer: I teach online classes for Grub Street.)

Past faculty: Charles Baxter, Colum McCann, Roxane Gay

Why you should go: It's a large conference with more than 800 people on some 100 panels. It's a good choice if you're looking to survey multiple sessions or want a conference aimed at all levels.

Highlights: The Muse draws a number of top New York agents and editors. For an extra fee, you can pitch them one on one by signing up for the popular Manuscript Mart. Don't miss the Shop Talk Happy Hour for guaranteed facetime with agents and editors if you're looking to land a book deal.

Where: Boston

When: May

Website: museandthemarketplace.com

2. The American Society of Journalists and Authors Conference (ASJA)

The ASJA conference is held each spring in New York City. Specifically aimed at freelance journalists and nonfiction authors, the conference attracts some 500–600 people each year. The two-day gathering focuses on helping independent writers survive and thrive as freelancers. Programs include pitch sessions with editors, agents and publishers. Can't make it to NYC? Regional conferences are typically held in the summer and fall in places like Chicago, San Francisco and Washington, DC.

Faculty: Speakers and attendees include editors and writers at *The Wall Street Journal, Newsweek, The New Republic, The New York Times Book Review, The Atlantic, Family Circle, BBC Travel,* Inc.com, *Fortune, Fast Company,* The Atavist, Seal Press and the Metropolitan Museum of Art.

Why you should go: This is the best conference for freelance journalists and those interested in pursuing a career as an independent writer.

Highlights: Networking with editors and other freelancers who understand what it is like to work for yourself.

Where: New York City

When: April or May

Website: asja.org/for-writers/annual-conference

3. San Francisco Writers' Conference

SFWC spans four days and hosts over 100 sessions including panels, two keynote lunches, workshops, networking events, open mic readings, and pitch sessions. You can pick from panels on everything from how to write a book, sell a book, get an agent or create a book proposal. The conference focuses primarily on the art of nonfiction and fiction books, but there are also panels on freelance and travel writing, to name a few.

Past faculty: Ann Packer, Jane Friedman, Annie Barrows

Why you should go: In addition to providing a great escape from mid-winter snow, this all-levels conference is ideal for first-time conference attendees looking to survey multiple panels.

Highlights: The conference always takes place at the InterContinental Mark Hopkins, one of the jewels of San Francisco, located atop Nob Hill. The luxury hotel provides elegant breakfasts, keynote luncheons and a gala. Each night, the conference hosts a group dinner at a different restaurant around town. They cost extra but are a great way to meet other writers and the presenters.

Where: San Francisco

When: February

Website: sfwriters.org

4. BinderCon

BinderCon is a professional development conference designed to empower women and gender nonconforming writers, authors and those in the media. An offshoot of the popular Facebook group Binders Full of Women, the main conference takes place in the fall in New York City with a second installment in Los Angeles each spring.

Past faculty: Lisa Kudrow, Jill Abramson, Anna Holmes, Leslie Jamison

Why you should go: You are a woman or identify as gender nonconforming and are interested in a writing conference that takes these issues into account.

Highlights: Drawing a lot of heavy hitters from the media world, including top women editors and agents, the conference abounds with the spirit of feminism. You're sure to meet some inspiring women.

Where and when: November in New York; February in Los Angeles

Website: bindercon.com

5. Literary Writers Conference

A two-day conference for fiction, poetry and creative nonfiction writers "learning how to maneuver in the marketplace." Hosted by the Community of Literary Magazines and Presses in conjunction with the National Book Foundation and The New School Graduate Writing Program, it attracts a number of prestigious editors, agents, publicists and publishers.

Past faculty: Michael Cunningham, Jonathan Galassi, Julie Barer, Gail Hochman, Renée Zuckerbrot

Why you should go: This is a serious conference for serious writers. Many panels include author-editor conversations, which are a fascinating listen for anyone interested in writing a book. Attendees are a mix of New School graduate students and mid-career New York writers looking for a book deal. It's small enough that it doesn't feel overwhelming and always has an impressive group of panelists.

Highlights: Agent speed dating. Each participant has the opportunity to sit down with two literary agents for eight minutes to pitch a book idea. Last year's event featured agents from Brandt & Hochman, Zoë Pagnamenta Agency, Kuhn Projects, Fletcher and Co., Trident, Folio Literary Management, Jean V. Naggar Literary Agency and Renée Zuckerbrot Literary Agency.

Where: New York City

When: November

Website: clmp.org/lwc

6. San Miguel Writers' Conference

This is a destination writers' conference where the atmosphere is just as important as the conference. San Miguel de Allende, a small town in Mexico, is known for its artistic community of writers, painters, musicians, poets and philosophers. In recent years, more American artists have flocked here in the winter.

Past faculty: Joyce Carol Oates, Gail Sheehy, Elizabeth Hay, Scott Simon, Juan Villoro

Why you should go: You have a sense of adventure and love the idea of mixing travel and writing. Perfect for those looking for an escape to Mexico during February.

Highlights: This conference draws famous media personalities in addition to some great faculty for the workshops. It is not just a literary conference, but also a cultural experience. Don't miss the live storytelling performances and the legendary fiesta, which Barbara Kingsolver has called "one of the ten best parties I've ever attended in my life."

Where: San Miguel de Allende, Mexico

When: February

Website: sanmiguelwritersconference.org

7. Sewanee Writers' Conference

The longest event on this list, spanning twelve days, Sewanee is built on a workshop model. Each participant is assigned a workshop that meets every other day, combining lectures and informal exchanges. Each one is led by two faculty members, but attendees can also meet with faculty one on one. The focus of this conference is on finishing submitted work, not generating new pages.

2016 faculty: Jill McCorkle, Alice McDermott, Robert Hass, Mark Jarman, Sidney Wade, Naomi Iizuka and Dan O'Brien

Why you should go: This conference is great for those looking for an immersive workshop experience with room and board included.

Where: Sewanee, Tennessee

When: July

Website: sewaneewriters.org/conference

8. VONA

The Voices of Our Nations Arts Foundation (VONA) was created in 1999 to address the lack of diversity in writing programs. The summer writing workshop offers two one-week sessions for up to 140 participants at the University of Miami. Workshops cover poetry, memoir and fiction as well as travel writing, speculative fiction, YA writing and playwriting. VONA also hosts regional weekend workshops aimed at specific issues.

2016 faculty: Tayari Jones, M. Evelina Galang, Willie Perdomo, Chitra Divakaruni, Minal Hajratwala

Why you should go: Those attending the multi-genre workshops tap into a larger community of support through the active VONA alumni network.

Where: Miami

When: June and July

Website: voicesatvona.org/workshops

9. The Bread Loaf Writers' Conference

The oldest writers' conference in America, and arguably the most prestigious, Bread Loaf was founded in 1926 by, among other notable names, Robert Frost.

Bread Loaf's main conference runs ten days each August and has been described as literary summer camp. But make no mistake: This is the big leagues. Last year alone, Bread Loaf received 2,100 applications for its 220 slots. Attendees study with one of twenty faculty members, each of whom offers a workshop. There are ten workshops in fiction, seven in poetry and three in nonfiction. Each participant submits a manuscript, for which he or she gets feedback during the conference.

2016 faculty: Patricia Hampl, David Shields, Natasha Trethewey, Lynn Freed

Why you should go: If you are serious about networking with contemporary writers and making friends in the literary world, this conference is for you. The schedule is jam-packed and very social, energizing participants to go back home and write. Don't miss the hayride, which is so popular it was featured in an episode of *The Simpsons*.

Where: Vermont

When: August

Website: middlebury.edu/bread-loaf-conferences

10. AWP Conference

The Association of Writers and Writing Programs (AWP) is one of the largest and most popular writing conferences in the world. With more than 15,000 annual participants and 800 exhibitors, it's more than a conference or book fair—it's an event. AWP is an essential experience for writers, students, teachers and academics alike.

Faculty: Everyone. If a writer has a book out or teaches often, chances are he or she will be attending.

Why you should go: This massive four-day event features 550 readings, panels and craft lectures from 2,000 participants. Everyone should go to AWP at least once.

Where: Location changes each year.

When: Spring; usually March or April

Website: awpwriter.org/awp_conference

Jennifer Mattson is a writer, journalist and online columnist at Psychology Today. *A former producer for CNN and NPR, she teaches writing at NYU School of Professional Studies and leads workshops around the country.*

Change Your Location, Change Your Luck: Residencies & Retreats

How else can winning writers log those 10,000 hours? Residencies are another great way to "get it done."

These "off-site" situations require applications and are often very competitive. I had the opportunity to judge one prestigious residency and was awed at the level of applicants' accomplishments. Many were post-PhD, with a number of books already to their credit.

Residencies vary widely. There is a class of retreat that offers the writer a place to stay and might charge a minimal amount. Others offer full room and board. The most sought after include a stipend or fellowship.

All offer solitude, but some residencies are organized to host nightly social groups, meals or critique sessions.

Retreats

While residencies require applications, a "self-directed" writing retreat is time away on your own time. Holing up in a friend's cabin, a hotel room, or vacation rental has produced some of the best writing. Some writers organize "retreats" with other writers, while some go it alone.

If you can cope with the idea of being alone for three to seven days, a self-directed retreat is an excellent way to add to those 10,000 hours.

The magic of retreats is that once you leave your routine, which might include breaking up your day with interruptions (car repair, doctor appointments, yoga, exercise class on a schedule, cat and dog care, child care, elder care etc.), you can "go with the flow" of your work.

What if the work is going slowly? Feel free to lie on the couch and look out the window for an hour. There's no one there to judge!

This article on creativity and boredom ran in the *San Francisco Chronicle* to much acclaim: "We try our best to avoid it, but boredom has its benefits. Today, it's a lost art form." It can be found at this link (active at the time of publication): https://www.sfgate.com/entertainment/article/ We-try-our-best-to-avoid-it-but-boredom-has-its-2799827. php

The series made the argument for the positive benefits of allowing ourselves unscheduled, empty time, especially regarding the creative process. In this series, the author argues, it is often through long stretches of solitude and quiet that the mind is able to create.

Author Karin Evans on her experience of writing retreats:

"Sometimes I didn't see them all day long, but I knew they were there. I'd go to the kitchen for a cup of coffee and see Sadia's toast crumbs on the counter, or I'd lift up the coffee pot and realize that Dan had already brewed a fresh pot, enough for the three of us. I had all the solitude I needed, but the quietude felt

richer and more promising than usual. As
I strung words and sentences together,
I felt companioned. I was alone but not
lonely. I knew that in distant private
corners of the house Sadia was writing her
poetry, interlacing beautiful words from
her native Somali language. I knew that
Dan was looking out over Tomales Bay and
writing about his favorite topic, salmon.
I steamed ahead on my own book, about
community, feeling perfectly supported and
encouraged by my invisible companions on
this writing retreat. By day's end, we'd all
wander into the common rooms, and compare
notes. The Mesa Refuge in Pt. Reyes Station,
California, gave us all the gift of time and
space to write for two wonderful weeks. It
also gave us an even more valuable gift—the
gift of each other."

How a Writing Retreat Saved Me

At one point in my career, I was convinced that I was finished. If it hadn't been for a writing retreat, I would not have finished my next two books. Here's the story:

The second phase of my working life (after a four-year stint in the exciting but cutthroat world of advertising) was in corporate sales. Self-discipline was critical to the success of my career. If I didn't make the daily cold calls, set up a schedule of appointments and diligently follow up with clients, I wouldn't make a living. Rain, shine, tired, not tired, I worked.

So, I learned the system of successful business people: "Plan your work and work your plan." I learned about focus and powering through and goal setting and self-imposed deadlines.

When I quit my corporate job to write full-time, I worked at home. And work I did. I was at my desk at 9:00 a.m. and sometimes long into the afternoon. I wrote my second novel, a book of short stories, and three poetry collections at home.

And then one fall the wind went out of my well-honed, self-disciplined sails. I couldn't get motivated. I felt isolated and uninspired. I found myself lolling in bed, reading and writing emails until after ten in the morning. I was easily distracted. And, I was convinced that I was finished. Had I possibly said everything I had to say? Was it time to think about another career?

While I was just beginning to struggle with the question of whether to go on or change careers yet again, I signed up for a writing retreat. I didn't know why I did it; I had never gone on an organized retreat before (see "Residencies and Retreats.") The retreat was ten days in Oaxaca, Mexico. I packed up my projects, projects for which I had taken notes, projects that had been languishing unfinished.

Every day, after breakfast, we eight writers retired to our rooms to write. And write I did. I started work on a memoir. I wrote new poems. The floodgates had opened. In the afternoons we would meet to talk about our process, have a teaching by our workshop leader, and share the work.

What changed?

Once I had a chance to work with and around other writers, I was reinvigorated. I was inspired. I was motivated again. I worked on a memoir, and on new poems.

When I got home, I realized I needed to be around other people. It was time for me to be working away from home. Out of the house. Away from the pet care and the home tasks. I had looked into renting an office space but the expense was always prohibitive. After all, I live in San Francisco.

A Note on Time Management

Time management is one of winning writers' biggest challenges. When you commit to a program of writing, submitting work, and networking, you will find time strangely shrinking—especially if you have a full-time job or children at home.

What I realized once I decided to become a winning writer was that time is a gift that you can give to yourself.

My college writing teacher, Kathleen Fraser, had a practice of committing Sundays to her own writing practice. As a mother, a college professor, and a community figure, she would never have written twelve books if she hadn't given herself that time.

There are shelves of books written on time management. If you find that you are trying but not getting the results you want from work, if you are having trouble getting on track, try reading one of those books for inspiration and guidance.

A Note on Taking Time Off

Only some months after that near-fatal autumn when I believed that my writing career was "finished," I realized that I wasn't finished at all. I was actually truly exhausted.

It had been a big year for both my family and my career. Early in the year, an agent I had been working with for a year (implementing her suggested changes, working closely on rewrites with her editor) rejected my second novel by email.

At the same time, my husband and I had started and completed a major remodel that had required many go-rounds with architects, structural engineers, designers, and vendors.

Our first child was planning a wedding, and I had completed a four-month pre-order campaign with Publishizer that included the creation of a "book trailer," a web page, and soliciting for over 260 pre-orders for my second novel.

"Knowledge work is tiring," my husband said. And tired I was. But when you are wired for hard driving, if you are a relentlessly hard worker, then the idea of rest is as strange as the sun rising at one in the morning. It just doesn't compute.

Still, sometimes, it is essential to the writer's well-being to plan in some rest time.

As we progress through the steps of *You Can Be a Winning Writer*, let's remember one adage from the Greeks:

Ars longa, vita brevis. Art is long. Life is short.

The point of this adage is that art takes time and life often doesn't give us the time we need. We often think we can finish our projects in a fraction of the time that is actually required.

Forewarned is forearmed. Give yourself time. Don't rush yourself or your projects!

You Wrote It. Now, Revise: Editing, Rewriting, & Working with Professional Editors

> Revise: "To alter something already written or printed, in order to make corrections, improve, or update."

An annoyingly vague definition for a creative project, right?

Where to alter? What to improve?

Revising is an art, an art as critical as the writing itself. Revising is a different skill than writing. This is not the skill of analogies, the senses, rhythm, timing, and drama, but one that requires the critical eye of an objective outsider.

The problem with editing your own work, however, is that editing is like examining the shortcomings of your own child: Hard, if not impossible to do. That's why a majority of writers employ outside editors.

Even if you do decide that you can distance yourself enough to edit your own work, remember that the critical eye of the editor is not the one you use while absorbed in writing a first draft. The first draft is when you are writing without judgement, hurrying to get down the thoughts and ideas that have been knocking around in your head, on paper, on sticky notes, or voice recordings—sometimes for years.

Virginia Woolf wrote, in her memoir *A Sketch of the Past*, on musing on writing about "reality" and reality—note the quotes: "Perhaps if I should revise and rewrite as I intend, I will make the question more exact; and worry out something by way of an answer."[2]

What Woolf is saying is that even while in the process of writing, she knew that changes needed to be made. Sadly, Woolf died before she did get to revising *A Sketch of the Past*, leaving her biographers and students of her work wondering about what exactly she did want to express.

A common practice of winning writers (Woolf among them) is to allow the manuscript in question to sit for a while. Turn your attention to other projects and let the one you just finished brew. Going back to your work after a period of time will give you a fresh perspective. Letting some time pass allows you time to get those critical editorial glasses on. Like a good pot of coffee—you wouldn't serve without brewing, right?

Don't forget: Finishing your first draft is an exhilarating moment. You've done what you set out to do. It is a moment to celebrate and to enjoy. For some, the hard part is over. For other writers the question lingers—did I nail what I wanted to say?

2   Janet Malcolm. *Forty-One False Starts: Essays on Artists and Writers*. New York: Farrar, Straus & Giroux, 2014.

Questions persist: How much to edit? How many times?

Most writers will engage in at least one or more revisions on their own. After allowing the manuscript to brew, they can see the passages that still need work, the descriptions that fell short, the plot points that were missed.

Think of your first draft as having carefully drawn the outline for a paint-by-number scene of the Swiss Alps. You've got the scale of the Matterhorn, the range of mountains surrounding the famous and dramatic peak. You've decided if it's spring, summer or winter. Are there villages below? Cows? A shepherd? Or are we in a ski resort? A famous hotel? What's the skeleton in the closet of that old villager? Was he a Nazi sympathizer? Did he harbor a Jewish woman in the war who he fell in love with and never forgot?

After your first draft, your job is to add color. Many writers even intentionally leave holes in their manuscripts, where they know they have skipped important facts in the interest of getting the story down.

You may decide in this draft to "pump up" the dramatic elements, or tone down the emotional intensity. And, oh, by the way, not every character always speaks with an exclamation mark! Can you say in three words what you just said in ten? Can you find the exact right word for the exact nuance of sentiment your character is feeling?

Example: Is it excoriate or chastise? Torpor or languor?

Did you get the usage correct? Is it inquire or enquire?

Sometimes even a poem can require four to five drafts as the writer checks and checks again for rhythm, meter, form, repeating words.

A note on grammar: Writing about writing is tough. On the one hand you want to be helpful and accessible. On the other hand, you want to be smart and sophisticated—you want to inspire readers. I love it when writing about writing makes the reader feel smart, and appeals to the genuine word lover. Silas House advises writers to stop talking about writing—or about not writing—and just get the work done. Silas advises to take time away from the chatter of conferences and the endless dithering of social media. "We must learn how to be still in our heads," he writes, "to achieve the sort of stillness that allows our senses to become heightened." The wonderful nonfiction writer Joyce Dyer refers to this as seeing like an animal.[3]

Hemingway was famous for writing at least ten drafts. For many writers, this is a respectable and expected task.

I've met authors whose first drafts are so unwieldy that they require major surgery—sometimes a complete rewrite. Other manuscripts need to be slashed by a hundred pages or more. This type of editing is not a small task, and it is challenging to do alone.

And how do these writers know their manuscripts need to be cut? Their early readers may have told them, or they may have realized after the manuscript sat for a bit that many passages were overlong, others not fully fleshed out.

---

3   Silas House. "The Art of Being Still." The New York Times. December 01, 2012. Accessed May 22, 2018. https://opinionator.blogs.nytimes.com/2012/12/01/the-art-of-being-still/.

When I finished the first draft of my second novel, I hired an editor. Katherine, an editor at a national magazine came highly recommended from a fellow writer. We worked on my book for over three years. That wasn't what I had had in mind, but it was what it took.

After working on my first novel, I knew what to expect when editing my second novel, but that still didn't soften the blows. After just a year, I was convinced that I had answered all of my editor's questions. I was ready to let it loose, to move on to other projects.

More than once I would head for a meeting confident that I was finished, only to be informed that there was still work to do. Those meetings often left me feeling defeated and discouraged. It would take me a few days, or sometimes even a week or two, to "get back on the horse," to face the manuscript again, to delve back into the story. I needed time to think about how to take a plot line further, a character deeper.

Finally, when Katherine did pronounce the book finished, I panicked. I was sure that it wasn't. We discussed the submission of the manuscript at length. She reassured me that I "could let an agent decide about any further changes." Katherine was intuiting my anxiety to let the book go. Writing is one thing. Going public is another. Of her own accord, she told me that she loved the book. When I fretted that it wasn't ready to be seen by agents, she shared a personal story: "My husband is a psychotherapist. He was writing a book. After eight years, I told him that his book wasn't ready. This is ready."

And then I made a terrible mistake. I sent my book to top New York agents to whom Katherine had gotten referrals.

When the work came back rejected from three agents, I was bereft. I had put everything I had into this book. I'd worked with—and paid—Katherine to midwife the book to perfection. How could this happen?

Katherine was nonplussed, convinced that we hadn't yet found the "right" agent.

Remember that I told you back in Chapter One that "I blew it?"

Here's the rest of the story: After being excoriated by the Pulitzer Prize-winning editor, I let my first novel go. Against Katherine's advice, I did not pursue finding "the right agent" but instead put the book aside—for five years! It was only later that I realized that the decision was a bad one. Only later did I realize that it was my lack of confidence that had kept me from revising the book and sending it back to the New York agent. Only later did I realize that her letter was not a flat-out rejection, but the beginning of a conversation.

A last note on working as your own editor:

"Kill your darlings" is such a common maxim of writing teachers that the expression was used to title a feature-length movie about the evolution of the Beat poet Allen Ginsberg. There couldn't have been a more classic case study of a writer who had to fight for the right to follow his passion to become a writer.

His mother suffered from mental illness. His father, had he had his way with his only son, could have completely commandeered his career, his decisions, and his emotional attention. His father wanted him to be anything but a writer.

At Columbia, Ginsberg met Jack Kerouac and William Burroughs. All were hell-bent on becoming writers.

"Kill your darlings" refers to the difficulty, challenge, and rigor of editing out the passages of the manuscript that you think are the coolest, but that a professional editor will often tell you are "off topic," "tangential," or, as my writing teacher once pronounced, "lost in the weeds." Killing your darlings is hard work. Many writers get attached to a quirky detail that doesn't serve the plot line or move the story forward. Can you trust yourself to be that tough?

From the iconic French author, Colette: "Sit down and put down everything that comes into your head and then you're a writer. But an author is one who can judge his own stuff's worth, without pity, and destroy most of it."[4]

A last note on hiring professional editors: Although writing programs such as Word have a grammar-checking function, it is far from perfect. A professional editor will check for grammar, proper word usage, plot, and character development. A professional editor's job is not to help you to feel good about your manuscript or to soothe your ego. She/he is reading with the sharp and inscrutable eyes of a publisher.

Are there alternatives to hiring a professional editor?

Some writers, strapped for cash, will ask a trusted friend to read their manuscript. I'm not a huge fan of this approach, if only because it can often produce unexpected tension. I recommend caution with this approach.

---

4   *Casual Chance*, 1964

A writer friend of mine doesn't trust editors. He insists that he is on the right track with his novel. Only the feedback from publishers and agents will tell. At our last meeting, his book was up to seven hundred pages.

Working with a professional editor can shield you from potential hazards: frustration and rejection.

At the same time, keep in mind that editors are subjective readers and each one will have a different opinion. Remember that the final word on your manuscript will come from the publisher's editors, so that even when committed to and working with a private editor, it is most likely that you will be going through a last revision with your publisher.

Financial Considerations

Editor's fees range widely. A good, experienced, professional editor will either charge by the hour (current rates are between $50 125/hour), by the page, or by the project. The industry standard at this writing is from $1,000–3,000 for a book-length manuscript.

Rates will often vary depending on whether the editor is reading as a line or copy editor or for plot flow and character.

A note on Max Perkins, the genius editor credited with discovering Ernest Hemingway, F. Scott Fitzgerald, and Thomas Wolfe: Initially, no one at Scribner except Perkins had liked *The Romantic Egotist*, the working title of Fitzgerald's first novel, and it was rejected. Even so, Perkins worked with Fitzgerald to revise the manuscript until it was accepted by the publishing house.

Its publication as *This Side of Paradise* (1920) marked the arrival of a new literary generation that would always be associated with Perkins.[5]

Perkins insisted on developing strong relationships with the authors that he took on. As an editor, he felt invested in the books that he was helping to shape. Take for example, Thomas Wolfe's saga *Look Homeward Angel*. Wolfe presented an unwieldy manuscript from which Perkins demanded a cut of 90,000 words. The process of compressing the book to a readable length was not easy and Perkins experienced a lot of pushback from the author.

You, too, can argue for your side and point of view, but at some point you will have to make the decision of whether to publish or not.

I will never forget one of my earliest experiences with a strong-fisted editor.

I had submitted a poem that included the line "under a-patchy-sky." I liked the double entendre of "a patchy" with "Apache." She wasn't buying.

I was twenty-two. I told her she didn't get my poem and I wasn't going to change it. The anthology from which I had withdrawn my poem went on to become a seminal feminist text anthology *No More Masks*.

---

5   "Maxwell Perkins." Wikipedia. May 14, 2018. Accessed May 21, 2018. https://en.wiki-pedia.org/wiki/Maxwell_Perkins.

It was after that when I began to accept the fact that, even if I was not in 100 percent in agreement with the editor, I would generally try to be open to his or her advice.

The movie *Genius* recounts the dramatic relationship of Perkins and Wolfe. You can see from Perkins' relationship with Wolfe that "killing your darlings" can sometimes be a highly charged emotional process.

Editors can surely make a writer's career. A perceptive editor can see the gem, the brilliance that sometimes even the writer herself cannot see.

The editor who took Anne Frank's diaries, Judith Jones, joined Knopf in 1957 as an assistant to Blanche Knopf. Jones worked mainly on translations of French works by writers such as Albert Camus and Jean-Paul Sartre. Before that she worked for Doubleday, first in New York City and then in Paris, where she discovered *The Diary of Anne Frank*.

Jones pulled the book out of the rejection pile. She later reported, "I came across Frank's work in a slush pile of material that had been rejected by other publishers. I was struck by a photograph of the girl on the cover of an advance copy of the French edition. I read it all day."

"When my boss returned, I told him, 'We have to publish this book.' He said, 'What? That book by that kid?' " She brought the diary to the attention of Doubleday's New York office. "I made the book quite important because I was so taken with it, and I felt it would have a real market in America. It's one of those seminal books that will never be forgotten," Jones has said.

Jones was an independently minded-editor on the level of Max Perkins who also championed Julia Child's cookbook. Quote from her: "It's funny, because the harder the books were to edit, the more challenging they were, the more fun, in a way. I always wanted to get to know the writer, because once they trust you, you work much better together."

Helpful or Harmful?

We've just spent the last pages discussing editors who nurtured writers' careers, discovered previously hidden talent, and brought deserving manuscripts to the public. For every Max Perkins who makes the history-changing decision, there are editors who hurt a writer's career, or at least deliver sufficiently injurious comments to wreak havoc with an established, or an aspiring, writer's self-esteem.

After my first novel came back from an agent with what I interpreted as a discouraging note ("You are clearly very talented. The second half falls down. Please tell us what you would like to do"), I hired a private editor. If the second half was falling down, I didn't know why. I had already worked with my writing teacher on the book and was sure it was finished. That Pulitzer Prize-winning novelist, working as an editor, tore my book to shreds:

"The female characters are male and the male characters are female. You don't go far enough with the woman's pain (the novel was the story of a kidnapping). A lot of writers learn how to write by writing their first novel. It's ok to put this one on the shelf. What else do you have?"

After a gulp (female characters male? Male characters female?), I launched into the story about my idea for my next novel that would be set in Silicon Valley. The idea of starting a new project was infinitely more appealing than the idea of bringing the first one to perfection for the New York agent. Career misstep number one.

It wasn't until after I paid said Pulitzer Prize-winning novelist $3,500 that I realized that she had neglected to provide a written report or a tape. There was no recording of the meeting whatsoever. Nor was my manuscript returned with notes.

The editor might not agree, but in retrospect, I see I was the victim of "Editors and Predators," a hard-to-define hazard in the writing world.

It's enough of a hazard that the Editors and Predators website warns writers against common pitfalls: editors, retreats, and conferences that promise important introductions, self-publishing scams, and even "agents" who charge a fee.

Another website in this space is Writer Beware.

One student came to me after she had paid over $4,000 to publish her historical novel. I was furious. The book was riddled with typos and poorly copy-edited. The publishing company also did not assist in marketing her book.

Also in the Editors and Predators vein are "book doctors." These are editors confident enough to market themselves as the "final step" before publication. They often cater to writers who have had one or more editors work on their book, and still have not won a contract.

While some book doctors might deliver what they prescribe, I again advise: Proceed with caution. A friend was told that she was "brilliant" and that her book (that she had labored over for ten years) was marketable. For the hefty fee of $10,000, they would "fix up" the book for publication. The book was never published.

You may wonder why I've just spent these pages on editors. I'm supposed to be teaching you how to become a winning writer, correct?

Correct. But there is an important aspect of the book world for which writers need to be prepared. You are responsible for delivering a clean manuscript with viable plot and narrative structure, and strong character development. There are no more Max Perkinses. The major houses have editors, yes, but not editors that have the time or resources to spend months— or even years—to help writers wrestle their manuscripts into saleable shape.

In the end, no matter how many revisions you go through, you may still not be at peace with the work:

Here is an article on "authors who hate their own books" (link active at the time of publication): http://lithub.com/13-writers-who-grew-to-hate-their-own-books/.

Managing Feedback & Working with Editors

Even if you do not aspire to a bestseller (we may all secretly harbor those dreams even if we don't publicly articulate them), most writers seek some quantity of validation and approval. For some writers of memoir, approval can mean simply the nod of the family. For many poets I know, self-publishing a book or two is gratification enough. These writers can often side-step the feedback process. The book is good enough for their taste, and that is what matters.

For others, only a book sold to a large publishing house will do. These writers will have to contend with many rounds of feedback. From early readers to editors, from editor to agent and from agent to publisher, the loop can often feel relentless, discouraging, and demoralizing.

As a young poet in my undergraduate days, my professors were vocal about their enthusiasm for my work. "Send this to the *New Yorker*!" one teacher advised. Did I send my work off to the *New Yorker*? No. I was intimidated. I was not confident.

After undergraduate school, I would occasionally submit work to magazines. In those days, we did not have Submittable, or online submission services. I labored over every package. I was working full-time. When one or two packages were returned, I deemed the work unworthy and forgot about submitting.

In graduate school, my professor, who had the good fortune to have her bestselling book *Norma Jean the Termite Queen* turned into a movie with Harvey Keitel, pronounced my book "cinematic." Did I send it off? No.

Finally, after graduate school, I sent it off. That's when I got the "you are talented" note from a well-known New York literary agent. That was also when I made the fatal error of listening to Ms. Pulitzer Prize-winning novelist and abandoned that novel in favor of writing a new one.

I reached a point in my career (after my second novel
was not picked up) where I felt betrayed. Betrayed by the
encouragement, by the praise. If I was so good, why had
I failed to sell two novels? Novels that were pronounced
"compelling," "cinematic," and "marketable"?

Mary Mackey, my dear friend and colleague, the author of
fourteen novels and seven collections of poetry, Harvard
grad and Sacramento State professor, confesses that she had
written five novels before she sold her first one.

You might wonder how I managed that stage of feeling
betrayed. Honestly? I vowed that I would stick it out. If I was
lucky and I found success, I would celebrate, but if I never had
a chance at success, I would not feel bitter or unhappy. I would
not regret the hours that I had devoted, the hard work, and the
money spent.

How did I move myself from disappointment to a place
of peace?

I sat with the disappointment. Literally. It was in meditation
that I was able to appreciate the moments of my life that
were joyous. I came to appreciate the ways that the writing
was an integral part of my life, and that, the two unpublished
novels notwithstanding, I had had over a hundred poems and
countless articles and reviews published and had garnered
over twenty writing awards. In the years since I had left the
corporate world to write full-time, I had had three well-
reviewed poetry collections and a book of short stories
published by respected small presses. While it wasn't exactly
what I had been hoping for, I had come closer to my goals.

I also realized that giving myself the time and space to write had opened up worlds of peace for me and that giving myself the chance had been the gift of my life. I had gotten a chance to express all that was built up inside of me, the chance for quiet and close observation, the chance to become an artist.

It was in meditation that I spoke to my teacher, the poet and writer Norman Fischer. Norman had graduated with an MFA in Creative Writing from the University of Iowa, the most esteemed creative writing program in the country. Iowa is famous for a majority of its graduates going on to work in Hollywood or as bestselling authors.

In a private talk, Norman told me: "The writing world is mercurial. I had a contract for a book I was really excited about. My editor left, the contract fell apart. You can't get too attached to these things. Besides, in the end," he said, "it is not where true happiness comes from. True happiness comes from yourself."

I also got support from other authors who had been through similar experiences. I read biographies of famous people who had faced severe challenges.

Feedback Loops: Friends, Family, Early Readers, & Writers' Groups

Have you ever seen the cartoon where a woman asks her husband, "Does this body make me look fat?"

Of course, if said husband wishes to remain married, chances are he quickly answers: "Of course not!"

Giving critical feedback is as challenging for friends and family to give as it is for us to absorb.

So where does that leave you with relying on friends and family as early readers? Perhaps, a way to approach this process is to keep it simple: Ask your early readers to read for flow and comprehension. Use this stage as a way to check if the very basics are working. Does the chapter flow work? Do characters develop organically? Do the scenes make sense? Tell your friends and family that you know it's hard to criticize, and not to worry: you are just asking for simple responses.

Okay, gentle feedback given. Check. Now you are ready for more.

The amount of feedback a writer is willing to take is directly tied to their personality, goals and ambitions. Emily Dickinson was prolific. The public believed that she had no ambition to publish, but later research proves otherwise. The ambition was there, the public recognition was not. Nevertheless, she persevered.

This section addresses the moment you decide to publish. At that point, you will be receiving feedback throughout the entire process! From the first drafts shown to family or friends, to the editor, from the editor to the agent or publisher, and from the publisher to the reviewer! From the reviewer to the prize committees!

Managing feedback is yet another hurdle or challenge inherent to becoming a winning writer. You have just committed X number of hours to your project. It's not a report you've written for your boss, an analysis, or legal brief. This is your life. Your heart and soul, your dream!

Statistic: Agents get 900 packages a *week* on their desks. Their job, and the readers in their offices' jobs (and their assistant agents' jobs) is to get those manuscripts off their desks as quickly as they possibly can. That's why "the first five pages" rule matters.

The story of Harry Potter: J. K. Rowling—alone—went on welfare to write the book. She wrote it in cafes and even in a bookstore in Porto, Portugal. She wrote anywhere she could find quiet. Her book was rejected repeatedly. Finally, her agent talked to Scholastic, a publisher that was on the skids. *The Weekly Reader*, its magazine sent to schoolchildren, was dying. They took a chance on Harry Potter. The point here: J. K. Rowling had to withstand many rejections and settle for a publisher whose reputation was sketchy. But the book caught fire with school children. As we say, the rest is history.

A Note on Time and Money

Asking people to read your book is difficult. For some people, asking a neighbor to pick up a quart of milk or a prescription when you are ill requires drawing from a shallow well of courage. Now you are asking people to read anywhere from fifty (the size of a full-length poetry collection) to three or four hundred pages.

The request, once you find the courage, can lead to disappointment.

A friend insisted that I show her my poetry manuscript. I knew she was a really busy person. "Are you sure?" I pressed. "Absolutely." This was a friend who was also writing a book— on women and ambition!

Three months later I asked her what she thought of the manuscript. She lashed out: "You shouldn't give people your work to read," she chastised.

"But you asked!"

"Well..."

Needless to say, I got what I paid for.

For myself, I am respectful of people's time. Unless I am 100 percent ready to reciprocate the favor, I will not ask a friend to read my manuscript. Or, I offer remuneration; payment, another sort of favor (cooking them a meal perhaps), or helping them with a trade—a number of negotiated hours of coaching time, helping them to become a winning writer.

I learned the value of early readers the hard way. When an agent asked how many people had read my novel, I was stopped short. I had to think long and hard about who I would ask. I will always remember those friends who volunteered, read the book, and gave me worthwhile feedback.

Another aspect of the feedback loop is the submission process. Consider yourself lucky if you receive a personal recommendation from the editor: "More imagery," or "Great poem but not for us" (which really can be true—each editor is seeking a specific aesthetic. For example, have you read the submission guidelines closely? Was the contest only for people from Kansas? Seriously. That's why editors advise: "Please read our journal before submitting.") If an editor publishes only formal poetry, and you send free verse, you are not going to win.

Many writers say that, if a piece comes back rejected, they use that opportunity to take a closer look. At that point, they might be motivated to do another revision.

And, yet, there might be a piece that you feel you have revised and honed and whittled down as far as you can. Then sit with it. And keep sending it. Because it might just be that you haven't found the right advocate. One writer I know says, "Unless a piece comes back a hundred times, I don't consider it unpublishable."

Enough Is Enough!

Another writer friend reports that when she sent her novel out, one publisher didn't like the first chapter, one didn't like the last! At what point do you stop taking feedback?

This might or might not be a record but my Silicon Valley novel had seven editors! I stayed open to new ideas, I kept improving it. As long as it keeps getting better, you know that you are still "in the creative process."

> *"Remember: when people tell you something's wrong or doesn't work for them, they are almost always right. When they tell you exactly what they think is wrong and how to fix it, they are almost always wrong."*
>
> —Neil Gaiman

On the other hand, I've been in workshops with people who can't take any amount of feedback; they are defensive, they push back on positive and negative comments alike.

As you can see, feedback is a tricky proposition. Certain situations (when you are confident in the work, for example) require that you stand your ground, or "keep your own counsel." Other times, some well-timed, well-received feedback can help you move that much closer to becoming a winning writer.

Endnote: I had written a short story that I believed had value, but had the sense that it was missing something. I showed it to a friend who added an historical detail that was just fantastic. *Paris Blue Redux* went on to win two fiction prizes!

"There are rules to writing a great novel. It's just no one knows what they are."

—Somerset Maugham

–Dos, Don'ts, & Challenges–

Do's And Don'ts

- Do vet your workshop leader. Research reviews, interview past students.

- Do make sure you are up to snuff on your grammar. Microsoft Word is not your editor! It is notorious for missing typos and grammatically incorrect language.

- Do read—everything you can: articles, fiction, poetry, nonfiction.

- Don't send your work to editors or agents until you are ready.

- Don't stay in a writing group of any kind if you are feeling unsupported and uninspired!

Challenges

- Show your work to a friend.

- Show your work to an editor.

- Offer something in return. If you can't pay, then cook them a meal. If you can't cook them a meal, take them on a picnic. Something nice!

- Set a goal for your writing. Is it twenty minutes per day or twenty pages per week?

Chapter 2

Commitment

Introduction

Nothing succeeds like persistence!

Motivational experts, Andrew Carnegie, and even Malcolm Gladwell's pop-science study of the 10,000 hours required to excel at any high-level skill, concur: The key to success is commitment.

The new age master Shakti Gawain added a different spin to the concept: Creative Visualization.

Creative Visualization borrowed from her predecessors: If you dream it, you can do it.

Visualization does not imply that success is a magic snap of the fingers. Gawain concurs with motivational experts: Achieving your writing goals requires a plan. She recommends activities such as mantras, meditation, and mapping.

A mantra might be: "Every day in every way I am getting better and better." "The present is a present." "My dreams are coming true."

Mapping might include a collage of your book's review in *The New York Times*, pictures of you on your book tour, or your book winning an award.

Her belief was "energy is everything," another spin on the power of positive thinking.

What does your commitment look like? Is it writing your 1,000 words in the quiet dark of morning before rushing to your day job?

Is it committing to a consistent schedule of submissions?

Is it putting a month aside every summer to do nothing but write?

Is it hiring a coach?

Or, is it going out of your way on a Sunday afternoon to bring a hot-off-the-press poem to an open mic, or to meet an author? Is it devoting an evening after work to networking, a night that you might rather prefer to go out with the guys or girlfriends?

Author Ann Gelder recounts how she broke the gargantuan task of novel writing into little pieces:

"Growing up, the bane of my existence was a loudly ticking orange kitchen timer. Every evening, my mother brought it into the living room and cranked it to twenty minutes—the length of time I had to practice the piano. During my frequent breaks, I stared imploringly as the timer's hash marks crept past the arrow, bringing me ever closer to release.

In early 2017, when the Trumpocalypse made writing (and everything) seem pointless, a friend suggested writing for just twenty minutes a day. I remembered that timer, how it embodied not only suffering, but the promise of its end.

And so, every morning, I wrote and/or stared at my laptop screen for twenty minutes—I gave myself credit for both. At first, the minutes dragged like hours. After some weeks had passed, though, I began to write for longer periods. Words flowed more easily. By December, to my surprise, I'd drafted a new novel.

As our national emergency intensifies, I fall back on the twenty-minute limit when I need to. It gives me a measure of peace, knowing that doing the minimum is still doing my work."

Some business people insist that a "stick-to-it" attitude produces results—even if they are not always what you expect! Here's another example of commitment from author Robin Klein:

"I'll be out, maybe at a lunch with friends. The day is seductively gorgeous as days can get—especially in California around April or May.

I'll be toying with the idea of how good a long hike or bike ride would feel. And then I realize that a bike ride, or hike, would take me away from my desk for three hours. And, I'm on a self-imposed deadline. So, I go back to my desk, wondering for just a moment if I am squandering a beautiful afternoon indoors.

Lo and behold—there's good news in my inbox. A request for me to present at a conference, an invitation to give a reading or to author a review. I'm not saying that invitation wouldn't be there a few hours

```
later—of course it would. But there's a way
that I feel rewarded for showing back up.
For myself."
```

I know an award-winning travel writer who has been flirting with finishing a memoir for over fifteen years. Recently she confided: "It's hard for me to sit at my desk when it's sunny. I get depressed if I have to sit and write." This writer and I live in California where we have over 250 days of sun a year.

What's your "weak spot"?

I'm going to take a leap and make an assumption about what separates winning writers from wannabe's: Winning writers do not equate taking time to build a writing career as a sacrifice, or even a task that takes them away from other "fun" things.

Author Joyce Thompson on commitment:

```
"I wrote an apprentice novel. My colleague
at Houghton Mifflin, where we worked entry-
level jobs, showed it to an editor at Dial
Press, who urged me to take time off work
and rewrite the manuscript. But I had no
idea how to rewrite then, so I waited until
another story came along and seduced me.
When I had six chapters and knew it was
alive, I went to my boss and said I was
pregnant with a book. She gave me a six-
week 'maternity' leave to finish the book. I
worked every day, all day and at the end,
had my first published novel, The Blue Chair.

For me, we're talking a forty–plus–year
```

```
commitment—sometimes feeling successful,
sometimes dissatisfied and aspiring,
always addicted to story and the dance
of language."
```

Deborah Cohen had a contract with a division of Random House to write a nonfiction book. Her advance was $180,000. This writer had worked long and hard on her proposal, had hired a coach, and sweated finding an agent. But now that she had the contract in hand, she was finding it terribly challenging to write the book. She was challenged beyond the normal procrastination; she was paralyzed, stuck.

Cohen decided that she couldn't write the book at home. She rented a small office. After some time spent searching for the perfect schedule to write the book, she sought out my guidance. "If you can see the quiet time, that time in your office as sacred space, *your* time, it might help you to focus. It's such a gift to have a few hours of quiet time. Use that time and write the book."

Over the course of writing the book, her high-school-aged son was in a terrible accident. She missed her deadline, but finally delivered the manuscript. She never did win another contract with that press, or any other press. I suspect it was her inability to deliver that may have affected her chance to become a winning writer.

For many writers, the prospect of a few hours of empty, alone space with a blank page is as terrifying as going in for major surgery. Even a writer with a contract.

"I stopped pretending to myself that I was anything other than what I was, and began to direct all my energy into finishing the only work that mattered to me."

—J. K. Rowling

I want to suggest that how you see your career—especially in the early days, before your first book is published, when, truth be told, no one really cares whether you write that book or not—is how you spin it.

I am convinced that the first book that is the hardest. Before anyone outside your family knows of your aspirations, before a publisher asks you to write a second book, before you begin to build your reputation.

A writer once said: "You have your whole life to write your first book and six months to write your second." Her reference was to her experience of selling her first novel, whereupon she was offered a two-book contract, provided she deliver the second book in six months.

How long you want "your whole life" to be is up to you. As we saw in the Craft section, entire books can be written in a month to six months. If your book is taking more than a year or two to finish, you might want to ask yourself: Is something holding me back?

Is taking the leap to commit to your writing career a sacrifice or a pleasure? Do you view it as gamble with low odds, or an opportunity? Is it building the foundation of your dream house, or do you worry that you might be wasting your time? And being truly honest with yourself, would you rather keep the "dream" of being a writer hidden away, or would you like to manifest the life you really want?

From award-winning author Mary Mackey:

"The two most important rules for writing a novel are: (1) revise, revise (2) never give up. Like everything else, I learned these rules the hard way. I wrote five novels before the sixth, *McCarthy's List*, launched my career when it was published by Doubleday and reviewed by *The New York Times*. Before Doubleday took *McCarthy's List*, it was rejected by every known publisher on the planet. I took it back, revised it twelve times on an IBM Selectric typewriter, which means I spent two years typing 4,200 pages until every line, every comma, every bit of plot, character, and setting were perfect. The revision paid off. *McCarthy's List* was not just twelve times better than those first five novels; it was fifty to a hundred times better. Now, when people ask me how many novels I've written, I say "fourteen," but the truth is I have written nineteen novels: fourteen published and five rough drafts."

In my early years as a writer, I was very happy to be a poet who occasionally saw her work in print. Once in a while, I was invited to read. I was working a full-time job and had committed myself to renovating a 1928 fixer-upper in Berkeley. In those early years, having a family and a home was my priority. It was not until later that I aspired to be a published author.

When my baby was born, I took a year off work. This would be the time when I began to identify more strongly as a writer. But once the year was up, I found myself working in non-writing jobs and writing at night. Publish? Who had time! Winning writer? Never going to happen.

Then I wrote my first novel. That was surely the time to get serious. It was one thing to write songs and poems. It made me happy! I was an artist, if only "on the side." But now, after committing hours and weekends, months, and finally years to a project, publishing seemed like the inevitable end to the arc of a long-term commitment. However, when push came to shove and publishing the novel became more of a challenge than I was ready to embrace, it was easier to go back to my other life, being a mom and working full-time. I would publish sometime, just not now.

From Meg Clayton, author of *The New York Times* bestseller *The Wednesday Sisters*:

> "There is no reason a married woman with children can't also be a committed artist. (This seems self-evident now but was not immediately clear to me.)"

If Not Now, When?

Abraham Joshua Heschel, the Jewish philosopher, asked this question. Interpret as you will, but the way I always read it was that "the time is now." "There is no tomorrow, only today."

Still, the time for proclaiming your commitment varies in each individual writer's life. I think that the time a writer—or any artist—makes the commitment to his or her craft and life dream is inextricably tied in to the level of confidence and self-esteem, as well as the willingness to manifest what he/she really desires.

To my mind, commitment to becoming a winning writer is not unlike a wedding vow, a pledge to one's lover or partner.

From poet and impresario Stephen Kopel:

"For myself, the impulse to commit, to make a commitment to writing from my heart, about my niece graduating from high school, meant that I had to be respectful of myself as an adult to make sure that whatever series of words 'comprising my writing' were worthy of her as a member of the Kopel clan.

I called superior string of words to elevate the thinking of an eighteen-year-old an appraisal on my part looking deep within that all of my experience of my life up to that point in time would be well served in regard to Celeste recognizing her uncle's infatuation.

Young people need to listen to their elders. Toward that particular end my commitment to her was both heart felt and lively minded.

Like a pledge commitment to a writing goal whether it is short or long term in nature is a promise to act with integrity and

YOU CAN BE A WINNING WRITER

with some degree of finesse in putting word
together.

In which she would find wisdom, familiarity
and a dollop of love.

As a committed poet, this writer offers a
grateful heart with a lifetime of reading
experiences and wanting to be a steward for
poetry for the moment and for the future.

This particular writer possesses an innate
gift for using our bounteous English
language that deserves craft, community
and commitment all in one humility
and humanity."

Diane's Story

My friend Diane is the founder of Blue Light Press, a small
publishing company. She is also a very committed poetry
teacher and a serious student of the cello. She has just
published the stunning first collection of a student, Pearl
Werbach. Pearl has studied with Diane for the past few years,
growing and maturing as a poet and writer. Pearl Werbach is
eleven years old! She is as serious as any adult we know about
becoming a poet.

Poetry gives her young life meaning and joy. I can see a clear
path of writing throughout her school years, going for her BA
in writing and her master's. I see Pearl as a winning writer,
one who will (hopefully) go on to accrue prizes and awards. I
see her having a fruitful career.

In my research for this book, I discovered that writers' choices span a lifetime—from eleven to eighty!

After meeting Pearl, I talked to writers who only decided to write in retirement. Writers might range from twenty-two to thirty, even thirty-five if they put off grad school for some years (remember, all creative writing or MFA grad schools require a body of work to apply.)

For some writers, like myself, the drive hits in mid-life.

How do you know you are experiencing an "If not now, when?" moment?

Author Kathleen McClung is a community college writing professor and poet:

"Building my writing career has been a complicated process. I've always been a voracious reader and wide-ranging writer—poems, stories, memoirs, skits, speeches, journalism, and other genres. After I finished my master's degree in English, however, I devoted most of my energy to teaching and editing. I focused on other people's writing. It wasn't until an editing job ended when I was forty-seven that I resumed my writing career with zest. I distinctly remember saying to myself, "Okay, now's the time to get serious." One of the most important actions I took at forty-seven was to sublet an office with a serene view of a garden. A room of my own, it's quiet, beautiful, and within walking distance of my home. Best of all, there are

no distractions or interruptions. Three days
a week I write here. For over ten years I've
savored sunlight streaming in the windows,
occasional birds, squirrels, cats—and once,
a skunk—in the garden, and my writing career
keeps humming along."

Where are you? Have you gotten your sea legs? Published a
few stories? Poems? A chapbook?

These are good markers if you are trying to make the
decision—and for many it is a long, arduous, BIG decision—
often the biggest one of their working lives.

A study released by the Bureau of Labor Statistics in 2017
reported that the average Baby Boomer held the highest
number of jobs over their lifetimes:

"Individuals born from 1957 to 1964 held an
average of 11.9 jobs from ages 18 to 50.
These baby boomers held an average of 5.5
jobs while ages 18 to 24. The average fell
to 4.5 jobs from ages 25 to 34, to 2.9 jobs
from ages 35 to 44, and to 1.7 jobs from
ages 45 to 50. Jobs that span more than one
age group were counted once in each age
group, so the overall average number of
jobs held from age 18 to age 50 is less than
the sum of the number of jobs across the
individual age groups."

The point I'm making is that our work lives have become more
fluid. This report cites an "average" number of jobs of 4.5

between 25 and 34. That means that half the workers changed jobs more than ten times between 25 and 34, some only twice. And even from 35 to 44, there was an average of three job changes.

What I'm saying is that, even if you did not head down the path of a writing career directly out of college, opportunities for career change are possible. The abundance of institutions, non-profits, and career and life coaches has also increased exponentially as the career change numbers increased.

Louise Nayer, a poet and author of *Retirement: From Anxiety to Zen*, writes:

When one woman I know retired, she said it was the first time in forty years that she actually looked at a red and gold leaf that had fallen to the ground. Another man said that when he retired, he took a walk in his neighborhood and gazed up at the Maple tree near his house, a tree that he had not looked at in decades. Retirement is a time to look closely. To write well, not only looking closely, but also using all the senses creates a rich world that readers can enter. Many people in retirement want to write about their pasts, to give to family members and/or to write stories that need to be told. What did the air smell like at a seaside vacation? What did the éclairs or napoleons taste like on the once a week dessert nights? Was the living room chair scratchy or soft? What did your Tabby cat's purring sound like? Or the sound of a thunderstorm on a trip back east? Retirement

```
is a time to not only delve into the past,
but to use all your senses to create
scintillating stories.
```

There are so many ways that writers start their careers. *The New Yorker* published a fascinating article on Late Bloomers which can be found at this link: https://www.newyorker.com/magazine/2008/10/20/late-bloomers-malcolm-gladwell

Of particular interest were the writers who were given the chance by a spouse, a partner, or a patron. Even the internationally renowned photographer Robert Mapplethorpe was only lifted out of poverty by a devout fan who became his life partner.

While accepting financial help, and even support and encouragement, can be challenging, by keeping the long view in mind, many writers can get through these difficult first years. Setting deadlines is one approach that can certainly help.

Poet and author Carol Smallwood, editor of *Writing After Retirement*, offers this anecdote from the book, in the chapter by Angela Narth:

```
"We are pleased to inform you that we love
your story for children and are most eager
to publish your book for our upcoming
season."

Is this a message you have been waiting to
receive? Well, it certainly was my dream
for the last few years before I retired
```

from a thirty-five-year career in education, and I was over the moon the day I received the long-awaited news that someone actually wanted to publish one of *my* stories!

What followed was a year and a half of editing, working with the illustrator, making required changes, approving format, compromising when disagreements arose, and conforming to tight deadlines. In 2000, eighteen months after the manuscript was accepted by GWEV Publishing, my first picture book for children, *Simon With Two Left Feet,* was published. Much to my surprise and delight, the book hit a nerve with the young reading public; it stayed on the local bestseller list for twenty-seven consecutive weeks. Over the next few years, it went into second printing, garnering: a Silver Mom's Choice Award, a Bronze Moonbeam International Medal, and short-listing for the McNally Robinson Book for Young People.

I walked around in a rosy mist after the book was released, visiting a number of bookstores to get a glimpse of *my* book on the shelves. By the time my head shrank back to its original size, I found I was involved in several months of whirlwind activity that left me happily exhausted. Q & A sessions following readings are typically about the book itself: the characters, the plot and so on. But there was one that the children were more interested in the business end of things such as: Who was my 'manager'? Shouldn't the bookstore charge more for my books? How long did it take to receive royalties? Could I claim my expenses?

Near the end of the session, one boy of about eight asked solemnly: "Are you an M?"

"An...M?" I echoed.

"From your writing," he sniffed. "You know, a millionaire."

He did not look impressed when I chuckled. He looked even less impressed when I pulled out the large poster-board pie chart that I had created in anticipation of such a question. As I began to pull the pie sections apart: this percentage for the illustrator, this percentage for the publisher, this much for the bookseller, and a so on, I watched as his face registered mild interest, then surprise. By the time the pie was reduced to the author's paltry earnings, his face was the picture of utter astonishment.

"Then why," he gasped. "Do you write books?"

And you must begin by asking yourself that very question. Since writing children's books is not likely going to make us rich, what is our compulsion to do it? Every writer will have a slightly different answer to this question. But the answers will likely center on the same theme: to affect children's lives in positive ways. And that is what children's books have the power to do: teach, touch, and inspire.

From novelist Deborah Chastene:

"Every year on the Academy Awards (which, I'll admit is the only awards show I watch all year), when the writing awards come on, my attention focuses like a dog hearing a fire engine's siren. How did he/she do it? Are they going to reveal their great and interesting back story?

And inevitably, said winning writer (of screenplay or adaptation of a novel to a screenplay) will, near tears, thank their husband or wife for believing in them enough to let them sit at home for two (or however many years) and pursue their dream.

And even then, some writers are not prepared. I know writers who have waited until after their first book is published to make the commitment to their writing full-time."

CR had written two historical fiction novels at the time we met. He had been through the wringer with one or more agents. Close to signing. Signing and then the agent didn't sell the book. He was working full-time at a non-profit, but writing was his calling. He had the soul of a writer. He had a master's degree in writing. He was a brilliant historian who grew up in Spain and California and was bilingual. Writing historical fiction was his passion. No, it was more than his passion; CR was convinced that this was his destiny. But how was it going to happen? He was really suffering around the time that I met him. He felt discouraged, disempowered and terribly frustrated.

With the help of two colleagues, CR started his own press. If Virginia Woolf could do it, why couldn't he? (And, *Chicken Soup for the Soul*, and....) By starting the press, he could publish his first novel without it being obvious that it was "self-published."

The press created a professional web page, contracted a host of authors, and had a respectable "list." A stroke of good luck landed a review of his book in Historical Novels Review.

That review catapulted his sales to 3,500—verifiable on Amazon. Within a year, he had an agent. He sold his next book and continued working at his full-time job. If he was going to quit his job, he needed backup. Thirteen years later, CR has just published his seventh novel and is signed with one of the top literary agencies in the country. Talk about a journey! CR was actively writing for over ten years before his first novel sold.

In the introduction to this book, I referenced an article in *Vanity Fair* that moved me to tears. It recounted the story of a Yale-educated writer and his sixteen-year journey to publication.

When I read the article, I felt for the first time that someone else had experienced what I had with my novel, *Fear to Shred*, about a Silicon Valley tech startup.

Chad Harbach wrote *The Art of Fielding*. His story paralleled mine, almost to a T. I had also put my book away—against my editor Katherine's advice—for seven years. When the tech world heated up, I worked on it again. I found a publisher.

That publisher and I worked together for a year, after which he decided to change his strategy and only publish screenplays!

At that moment, I suffered a severe setback. At the time when the publisher for *Fear to Shred*, my second novel, offered me a contract, I had been about to sign a three-book contract for short stories. The negotiations had dragged on for almost a year. When that publisher learned that I had signed a contract for my novel, she pulled the contract.

All told, I had just lost contracts for four books.

But I was a winning writer, right? I admit, I wasn't feeling too winning for about a month. I was shell-shocked. Then a friend referred me to her agent. I worked with her for a year. She rejected my Silicon Valley novel via email.

I put the book aside—again! But this time, fortunately, for just a few months. Three months after the email rejection, Publishizer called me. Reticent at first, I agreed to design a pre-order campaign and work with them. Publishizer insists that they are not a literary agency, because their model is to support the writer. But they are the people who often make the connections. The Publishizer model is to support authors to design a "pre-order" campaign. Once the author has five hundred pre-orders in house, they present the author to publishers.

The campaign was very hard. At the time, Hillary Clinton was campaigning for President. I felt her pain! I was deep into campaigning; I was out talking to people every day, working on creative ways to get to my pre-orders. I hired a video artist to create a trailer for the book. I wrote and rewrote my synopsis. Designing and completing the campaign took six months. The novel made the rounds of publishers. I waited a year. And then I found a publisher that I really liked.

That Silicon Valley novel? From first draft to sale? Seventeen long years. Just like Chad Harbach.

The Story of *The Long Blue Room*

The Long Blue Room, my most successful collection of poetry, went through four full iterations. Its first title was *Senses*. When it didn't get picked up, I went back and edited, added and subtracted poems. I retitled it *Behind the Veil*. I sent the manuscript back out. I submitted to contests. Nothing. I changed the title again: *Scraping Dead Stars Off the Pavement*. I was getting nervous. Thirty poems in the collection had been published, three more than twice, and seven had won awards. It had been four years since my previous collection, *A Dreamer's Guide to Cities and Streams* had been published.

One Sunday afternoon, I drove out to a popular reading series about forty minutes away. I like to spend Sunday afternoons at home. My husband works full-time, and travels throughout the month for work. Sometimes, an entire week can go by where we both have after-work commitments and we don't see each other. So, Sundays are kind of a sacred time; a day for hiking, managing house repairs, making plans for travel, or hanging out with our friends or our adult children.

Sunday is also a day when writers get together. So off I went.

At the open mic, I read a poem that had just been published in an anthology, *I Know Why Sylvia Plath Put Her Head in the Oven*. It is a strong poem, but I wasn't sure it was the exact right choice for a sunny Sunday afternoon. Still, I was excited about it after the anthology had received a great review in which the writer had singled out my poem as a "drop dead gorgeous page poem."

After the reading, a woman introduced herself to me. She took my card and said she wanted me to meet some people who were looking for manuscripts.

The people she wanted to introduce me to turned out to be my next publisher, Benicia Literary Arts. And *that* is how my most successful collection was published. Of course, this story overlaps with "Community," but the point here is that, by sticking with the manuscript, by believing in it, by "putting myself out there," the book finally received the attention it deserved. Total time from having a manuscript ready to publication: three years.

Surviving a Drought

We Californians know a lot about surviving a drought. We cut back on water usage, hop in for a quick shower, turn the water off while brushing teeth. We turn our lawn sprinklers off, let the grass go brown, or put in drought-tolerant plants. And we pray!

How do you survive a publishing drought?

How do you live through a year of not having a poem, article, or story accepted? Two years of rejection on your manuscript, novel, or book proposal? How do you get through without giving in to self-doubt and despair?

If there is a ubiquitous phrase among writers, it has to be, "I'm not good enough."

Writer's Toolkit

1. Remember that responses to your work are subjective. You keep going until you find your champion (remember *The Art of Fielding*).

2. Have alternative ways of adding publication credits: Write a review. Author an article. If you are sending out stories, try a flash fiction piece. If you are sending out a novel, try to send out a short story.

3. Get support. Like Kay Ryan and Jane Hirshfield, get a buddy. Even if you both complain once in a while, chances are you will be able to buoy each other up.

4. Go to events. Keep meeting people. You don't have to necessarily tell people you meet that you are in a drought, but, as with my reading at the café, you never know who you will meet.

A Note on Passion

Once in a while, when I'm out socializing, I mix it up with aspiring writers. On hearing that I coach writers, someone will inevitably confide: "I want to be a writer." "Oh, really?" "Yes, but I can't seem to do it."

If I had to parse this sentiment (deconstruct, decode, decipher), I would offer the following advice:

Do you want to, but you are not ready to face the fear (of the blank page, of rejection)? Or, perhaps you know other writers, and so you know how much work is involved. Maybe I know a fast route or another secret? A shortcut?

The first task I would assign is to do what I call a "big think." My "big think" might be your soul searching or meditating. Either way, committing to what could turn out to be a years-long project deserves serious consideration.

Questions

Are you really passionate about your project?

Are you passionate, but fear is in your way?

I'd like to make a distinction here. Many people enjoy the process of writing. They are daily or weekly journal writers. They write a letter to the editor. They even write an opinion piece or a review or an article.

That's wonderful! Writing is a superb way to keep in touch with your thoughts and feelings. There's a difference between writing this way and becoming a winning writer. A winning writer is driven. A winning writer wants to make a career out of his/her writing.

From *Drive* by Daniel Pink:

> "As Carol Dweck says, 'Effort is one of
> the things that gives meaning to life.
> Effort means you care about something,
> that something is important to you and you
> are willing to work for it. It would be

> an impoverished existence if you were not
> willing to value things and commit yourself
> to working toward them.' "

There is effort and then there is passion. How does passion tie into commitment?

There was a man in my writing workshop once who wrote very bland prose. My teacher asked if he cared about what happened to his characters. I held my breath. I thought that was a pretty bold question. "Not really," the writer responded. "Well, if you don't care about them, how can you expect your readers to care?"

It's the same with getting to your desk, going to that event on a Sunday, pushing yourself out of your comfort zone. There's passion behind that drive. The passion to tell your truth, to share your personal viewpoint, to tell it loud and tell it proud.

From award-winning author and Brown professor, Ann Harleman:

> "How lucky we writers are! Commitment's
> rewards are always double. Art gives meaning
> to life, and life gives heart to art. *It's
> all material!* we remind each other when bad
> things happen.
>
> Meeting my first love a decade after he broke
> my heart, the old cruel desire scrolling
> down my spine. The burglar I surprised at
> midnight, a nylon stocking pulled over
> his face, prying up my living room window
> with a crowbar. The time I was bathing my

```
terminally ill husband and he slithered—all
two hundred pounds of him—out of my grasp,
and I had to call the Fire Department to get
him out of the bathtub. Cutting the pearly
fingernails of my red, wriggling, day—old
grandson because my daughter couldn't bear
her firstborn tears.

I've spun that straw into gold.

My next novel, getting nearer by the day,
will show me what my husband's death can
teach me about grief, about loss. At the
same time, it will let me revisit Bruce as
he was, in all the ways he was, the sight
and sound and feel and smell and taste of
him. There's no better comfort than that."
```

At the Northern California Book Awards in 2017, an award was given to one of the founding members of the Black Panthers.

"I was an engineer," he told the audience. "A working, middle-class guy. But we knew things had to change. So, we said, we're going to get some guns. We had no intention of killing or even harming anyone. We just were tired and wanted attention for our cause."

Think of becoming a winning writer like that. You can't sit idly by and wait for it to happen. You have to make it happen.

Building Your Writer's Resume

David Buuck lives in Oakland, CA. He is the co-founder and editor of *Tripwire: A Journal of Poetics*, and founder of BARGE, the Bay Area Research Group in Enviro-aesthetics. Recent books include *Noise in the Face of* (Roof Books 2016), *Site Cite City* (Futurepoem, 2015) and *An Army of Lovers*, co-written with Juliana Spahr (City Lights, 2013). A new chapbook, *The Riotous Outside*, is forthcoming from *Commune Editions* this year.

Zoe Tuck was born in Texas, became a person in California, and now lives in Massachusetts. She is pursuing a PhD at UMass Amherst and co-curates the But Also house reading series. Since the publication of her book, *Terror Matrix*, by Timeless, Infinite Light, Zoe has been a member of the press's editorial collective, as well as being a co-editor of *HOLD: A Journal*. She is currently working on a new poetry manuscript and a critical work about transgender poetics.

The Poetry Project

131 E 10th St, New York, NY

General admission: $8

Students/Seniors: $7

Members: $5 or free

No one is turned away for inability to pay.

Notice something interesting in these two short bios?

Both writers are performing in New York. Neither is from New York. They were invited by the Poetry Project as writers of import. Yes, they are both authors of at least ONE book. But what else do these two writers hold in common? Both are active in their respective communities. Both are volunteering their precious time (and precious it is when you are pursuing a PhD). These one-paragraph "statements" are not author's statements. They are not treatises on your aesthetic vision or your mentors or scholarship. They are telling the world that you are active in the literary world, and that your care, time, and attention are focused on a big picture, not simply your own career.

Involvement in the community is a sort of code for, "I'm a person who can be trusted. I am not just for myself, but I stand for literature as a whole."

Notice something else? The Poetry Project, the group that invited them, is *charging* to hear them. How about that?

Your writer's resume is your calling card to publishers. It differs from a work resume in that it is not linear, nor salary-based. Your writer's resume is a report card to publishing professionals (Acquiring Editors, Publishers and Literary Agents), detailing where you stand in your literary career. It lets these professionals know that you have already begun to build a history of success with your writing.

You start with three paragraphs in your cover letter. The first is an introduction:

Thank you for the opportunity to submit to your prestigious journal. I've read back issues and think that my work would be a good fit.

The second paragraph is a list of the poems that you are submitting.

The third paragraph includes your most prestigious publications, a line or two about work you do that is literature-related (even if it's volunteer), and perhaps a line about your education or day job.

Why is this third paragraph so critical an aspect of your cover letter that we are dedicating an entire section of *You Can Be a Winning Writer* to it?

Your publications tell editors and publishers that you have been vetted by other editors and publishers. The harsher the critic, the more the current prospective editor or publisher feels vindicated in the decision to accept your work. It's akin to a referral, a word-of-mouth connection, an introduction.

Starting from Scratch

Building your writer's resume is not a step that winning writers skip. Yet, if you are just starting out, what can you say? Scroll through your mental Rolodex, your writing files. Did you publish an article in your college journal? What about your blog or an article for the local paper? If you don't have any publications, get busy.

Write a book review or two and submit them to online magazines. In recent years, magazines, journals, and blogs, strapped for cash, have let full-time reviewers go. While they might not have the resources for paid reviewers, they are hungry for content. Chances are you'll start racking up publication credits quickly.

Start small.

Think global, act local. Who is the editor of the local press, the community magazines, or the state or regional writer's guilds that are publishing anthologies? Many states have poetry societies, a local poet laureate. Universities almost always have a literary magazine for their English departments. These are great places to get started.

From author Joyce Thompson:

> "I started writing poems at ten, took a couple of college workshops during high school summers, had my first little mag publication just before my eighteenth birthday. From poems, I moved on to short stories, then at twenty-two, my first novel. Small is always good—it permits experimentation and that fuels growth."

The next level to pursue is online publishing. Can you write a guest post for a popular blogger? Or, how about pitching a story to an online magazine?

What about the line in your third paragraph regarding your activity in the literary community? Starting is as easy as volunteering at the local library, tutoring for an after-school reading or literacy program. You can offer to teach writing basics to schoolchildren or at senior centers, or for a writing organization such as PEN, The Women's National Book Association, or one of the myriad organizations that organize and support writers.

To continue to the next level, begin reading and researching literary magazines and journals in your genre. Check submissions dates and policies and send them work. Even if you don't have a story or a group of poems ready, you can submit a review, an essay, or an article on a current event or socially relevant topic.

There are many services that assist writers. They research appropriate publications, locate editors' names and determine submission dates and policies. Some of my favorites are in the back in the resources section.

Your goal in your first years of establishing yourself as a winning writer is to build that writer's resume to catch an editor's attention. You don't want to come up empty-handed when an agent or publisher asks, "Have you published fiction before?"

Remember, success builds on success. Once you have a strong paragraph on your cover letter, branch out. Go bigger. You may not have been confident enough to submit to the *New Yorker* during this building period, but you might now.

Literary journals are tiered according to their circulation numbers. There are the small mags published by college MFA programs (circulation usually under 5,000); after that are the literary journals and magazines that are nationally distributed and have a solid readership (5,000–20,000). The last are the top tier that are scoured by agents and publishers. Some names here include *Rattle*, *Prairie Schooner*, *Poetry*, and *Boulevard*.

The *crème de la crème* are the magazines with the largest circulation numbers: the *Atlantic*, the *New Yorker*, the *Paris Review*.

Note: If, during this building period, you pen a real gem (your writing workshop or teacher tells you it's so fabulous, really outstanding), then go for it! Send it to a top journal. Mix it up! There is a phenomenon called an "outlier."

Outliers

These are the books, screenplays, poetry collections that defy common practices. They rise to the top. The author has a finger on the *zeitgeist*, or the writing stands out in a way that grabs a publisher's attention. It does happen, and it can happen to you. My philosophy is, "Hope for the best. Plan for the worst."

Here, for your reference, is a sample cover letter that won three publication credits.

JOAN GELFAND

23 Bluebird Way
San Francisco, CA 92569

joan@joangelfand.com

May 29, 2018

Connecticut Review

Dear Editors:

In response to your call for submissions for the Connecticut
Poetry Society, I have enclosed three new poems
for consideration:

Peonies
Praying at the Altar of Nam June Paik
Foreign Seductions

The author of three well-reviewed collections of poetry and
an award-winning chapbook of short fiction, my work has
appeared or is forthcoming in: *Kalliope, Prairie Schooner,
Rattle, Levure Littéraire, The Meridian Anthology of
Contemporary Poetry, Chicken Soup for the Soul*, and many
other anthologies and journals.

I am the Development Chair for the Women's National Book
Association, a member of the National Book Critics Circle and
Bay Area Travel Writers. My blogs appear regularly in the
Huffington Post.

I hope you enjoy the poems.

Sincerely,

Joan Gelfand

My friend and colleague Dr. Andy Jones, AKA Dr. Andy, calls building your writer's resume "climbing the staircase." Climbing it is. As I've outlined, you start small, gaining altitude and elevation as you progress.

Getting Published is like Looking for a Job

Sadly, your success in your field of work will have little impact on doors opening to you in the literary world. I know doctors, attorneys, and venture capitalists who have struggled with building a writer's resume, getting published, and establishing a literary career.

Every writer is judged on the same criteria: the writing, the relevance, and the writer's resume.

And, don't forget, even winning writers can experience backslides. Their fortunes turn. Some writers enjoy a wild ride; two steps forward, then one back. Having success and stalling is not uncommon.

Jackie's story:

Jackie was lucky. A darling of our MFA poetry program, Jackie's first book of poems won a prestigious award. Her next book won another award, and her third book also won an award.

She was employed at a private college, teaching writing. Steadily, Jackie moved up the ladder to full professor. It took about ten years, but, by the time we re-met after being classmates, she was teaching creative writing at two colleges.

And then her fourth book hit a wall. Her editor at her former publishers demeaned her new work. Contests and awards came up empty-handed. She sent her manuscript out for over two years. She began to doubt her work. "Narrative poetry is dead," she worried.

Frustrated, she sought the advice of fellow poets. I told her my story (see below: Think outside the box), but it was the advice of a local, very successful, award-winning poet that helped to get her book published. "Forget the contests," he told her. "Submit to publishers' open reading periods." Within six months, she had a contract for her fourth book. While she was disappointed not to win a prize, and while the process had shaken her confidence and forced her to question her relevance, she survived this bump by going back to the basics of the Four C's of successful authors.

She never stopped writing and honing her craft. She continued to submit, committed to the process. And, although it was a challenge, she remained confident. In the end, her connection to community was the deciding factor.

A note on context and the business climate: During the period when Jackie was submitting her fourth manuscript, the publishing world was experiencing a sea change. Publishers were folding (statistic 2013–2016[6]), digital publishing was disrupting traditional publishing and the country was coming off of an economic disaster. On top of these adversities,

---

6   "Global Trends in Publishing" by R. Wischenbart. Accessed at http://wischenbart. com/booklab/?p=599.

the competition had grown significantly stiffer, thanks to a proliferation of MFA programs.

"During the first six months of 2014, trade print book sales are estimated to have declined between 25 and 30 percent. Bookstores report that, due to a huge drop in consumer spending, book sales have stagnated. The total sales loss since the beginning of the crisis, back in 2008, amounts to some €700 million in just four years."

Wischenbart further explains:

"E-books and digitization are just two of many disruptive elements. Even before the emergence of a significant market for e-books, a sea change in the traditional retail business resulted in a shift towards online sales."

Persistence: The Inside Story

From Joan Lester, author of *Black, White, Other*:

```
"I've got a nibble!" My agent Caryn bubbled
through the phone.

"Yay!"

"The editor at…" Caryn paused and named a
major publisher. "Loves it. But he wants a
rewrite."

"Before contract?"

"Yeah."
```

I'd been down this path before. Three times editors had gushed to Caryn about how much they adored the manuscript for my young adult novel, a first children's book after three nonfiction adult books. But each had demanded revisions before offering a contract, and as soon as I completed new drafts, their enthusiasm disappeared. "The seams show," one complained. "We've just acquired another biracial novel," a second said. And a third hardly explained what she no longer loved.

By now, Caryn had sent the manuscript to forty-three houses. We were midway into the fourth year of submissions. And although she kept reassuring me that she was 100 percent committed, I didn't know how long she'd have the patience to keep investing time in this project. And would I? Each rejection triggered doubts: Am I really a writer? Do I have the skill to find the right structure, the voice? Maybe my career is over, I worried. My lack of a sale fueled an insecurity common to women, who've not been as well published as men.

Now that we had a nibble, did I dare refuse the latest editor's request for a rewrite? I'd seen that each revision brought a clearer vision; the manuscript grew steadily better. This editor declared five times to Caryn how much he LOVED my manuscript—which was heartening. But he also insisted that since I had no track record in children's books, he needed to see how good I was at revisions before he made an offer.

Discouraged as I'd grown about my ability to rewrite to specification, I was afraid to get hopes up again without any guarantee of publication.

"No," I told Caryn.

Seven years of sweat and heart had gone into this project. What kept me going through the rejections? My agent's encouragement, along with that of writer-partners and my wife, certainly buoyed me. But above all it was my own joy in the writing process itself: simply forming sentences, lying in bed at night struggling to find the perfect word, the satisfying arc. Mulling over favorite paragraphs, or the whole story itself. That pleasure battled the demoralization that sometimes engulfed me.

Caryn kept submitting. Until a day arrived that I thought I'd never see. "An editor is ready to make an offer," she said. "The editor wants revisions, but is willing to have you do it *after* contract."

I signed.

And I did revise, under the guidance of a terrific editor. After *Black, White, Other* came out in 2011 the publisher, HarperCollins, promoted the hell out of it, sending me repeatedly on publicity tours. In 2012, they put out a paperback edition, and, to my surprise, in 2016 published a third edition with a new imprint, Blink, creating yet another gorgeous cover. After all that waiting, this turned out to be the perfect publisher.

Not long after, I had a similar experience with an adult novel, *Mama's Child*, which began as a memoir. But after six years of rewrites—alternating with revisions of *Black, White, Other*—and no agent willing to take it on, the book found its right form only when it morphed into a novel. With the freedom that fiction allowed I was able, at last, to imagine my way into a successful story and the enthusiastic support of an agent. Once she sent it out for submission, Atria/Simon and Schuster, the publisher of an earlier nonfiction book of mine, snapped it up.

"Old age is not for sissies," Bette Davis is reputed to have said. The same goes for the writing profession. We must be tough enough to weather rejections, endless rewrites, and long periods—often years—when we're muddling through, waiting for the writing to jell. But if we accept the inevitable fact that projects take time to emerge into their best shape, we can settle into the pleasure of the writing itself. And ultimately, the sweet feel of a book brought to successful completion can be ours to savor."

Why else is getting published like looking for a job?

If you were starting out, you wouldn't stop at one interview, would you?

You would research companies that matched your skills; you would target specific companies. You might even sign up with recruiters.

Above all, you would continue to improve your skills in the field in which you were seeking employment. You would take classes, you would network, you might go to conferences and workshops to network.

"I wrote a book. It sucked. I wrote nine more books. They sucked, too. Meanwhile, I read every single thing I could find on publishing and writing, went to conferences, joined professional organizations, hooked up with fellow writers in critique groups, and didn't give up. Then I wrote one more book."

—Beth Revis

Treat your writing career like that.

Put your best foot forward.

In the work world, it's your resume; in the writing world, it's your cover letter.

Becoming a winning writer is serious business. People are busy! Remember, agents receive 900 packages a week on their desks.

And, not everyone starts their career off with their dream job. Some start in the mailroom and move up.

Internationally published journalist Deborah
Grossman writes:

"In the beginning, there was hope. I took
writing classes and attended workshops.
A few months later, a regional newspaper
published my essay about racing through life
until I drove into the reality of turning
fifty.

I read writers' magazines and sent out
queries. I religiously jotted down ideas and
forged them into queries modeled by workshop
leaders. Stacks of envelopes hit the mailbox
and outbox. Editors ignored or rejected my
ideas. My self-image as a writer was fading.

After twenty years as a corporate manager,
I was struggling to rev up a second career
as a freelance journalist. One day while
talking to my good friend Max from my
corporate life, I mentioned my frustration
in getting anyone's attention. Max had left
the company a few years earlier and turned
her energy into making jewelry with great
success. She told me something very simple
and very profound.

At first, she had encountered the same
lack of interest for placements. 'I had
to branch out and sell my products to an
entirely different set of stores,' she said.
'Eventually I found people who liked and
appreciated my work, and you will, too.'

She was right. I reframed my freelance

experience: If the fit isn't there with one publication, for whatever reason, query a variety of other outlets. *In lieu of feeling dejected and rejected, I simply envisioned myself barking up the wrong tree. Someone will get what I'm doing.*

I went on to attend writers' conferences and asked many writers for their recipe for success. I've found great satisfaction in a creative, adventurous career. After writing for newspapers, I focus on magazines and websites with international audiences. I travel widely to discover global tables with interesting food and drink stories to serve up for readers."

Prizes, Awards, & Money

Money is a personal, and often loaded, issue. Writers seem to fall into one of two categories:

1. Spending money on your writing career is an investment in your work.

2. There is no good reason to spend your own money on your writing career.

While there are many free contests, awards, and fellowships for which you can apply, there are also contests for which you might want to consider that charge a fee. Free or fee, competition is stiff.

YOU CAN BE A WINNING WRITER

I like to think of spending money on my writing as like buying that expensive interview suit: I might never wear it out to dinner, but it looks great!

Contests

Fees range from free to as little as $5 and as costly as $50. The odds are stiffer than ordinary submissions, but a contest win shines on your writer's resume like glitter. Think of a contest or award as the bling of your writing career. It's not something that comes along every day, but is very special.

Contest and awards odds may be slim, but so is the lottery. Someone has to win, right? Unlike the lottery, winning a contest can build your reputation in far-reaching ways. Winning a contest or award from a chapter of PEN, a university, or a writer's guild will expose your work to a national audience. Winning awards for online publications can increase your international reach.

Winning a highly sought-after contest (the Rona Jaffe award for fiction) won Christina Nichol her agent, and eventually led to the publication of her award-winning novel about the country of Georgia, "Waiting for the Electricity." Christina also had a journey she didn't expect with her book: Her agent had a terrible time placing it. After forty rejections, Christina met an editor who championed her book, and, she won the California book award from the Commonwealth Club.

One of her rejections (from a renowned publisher who shall not be named) was an unnecessary but not uncommon insult: "Your book is manic and relentless." How would you like to add that one to your file of no-thank-yous?

Personally, I'm a big fan of contests and awards. As with your other submissions, once you win your first contest or award, your confidence increases. Suddenly the world of contests and awards doesn't seem as random.

For, as much as I recommend a regular program of submissions, there was a time when I did not follow my own advice. My mother had been ill, a friend's daughter was in crisis, and I was struggling with a revision of my novel. I had fallen down on my own submission program. But in my file was a contest that called to me.

"Fiction chapbook contest. Send us three stories. $25 entry fee." I recognized the press name because I had just reviewed a colleague's book from that very same publisher.

I organized a file with the three stories: One that had won an award from a well-regarded literary journal, one that my writing teacher had raved about, and a third story that had been published once. I forgot all about the contest until I got a call from the publisher that I had won. It was an international contest with stiff competition. And it was a fluke. There were no percentages to compare against. I had submitted once in a three-month period and won.

For winning, I received twenty-five complimentary copies and was invited to read at an art gallery in Boston, hosted by the publisher. At the reading, I met local Boston-area writers who became friends.

Yes, the win was a fluke, but if I hadn't thrown my hat into the ring with that submission, I would have missed out on a very good opportunity.

There's a wonderful saying that speaks to luck: The harder I work, the luckier I get.

Post-Publication Book Awards

Post-publication awards are the prizes that you are eligible to apply for after your book is published. The Pulitzer, National Book Award, National Book Critics Circle, and PEN are all post-publication awards.

Tip

Your new book has an arc and a life. When the book is first published, you are lucky if you receive a few well-placed reviews. The reviews will help your new book to get noticed and will increase sales. Sales are managed by the publisher and its marketing team, and by you as an author. Post-publication awards can give your book new life. Consider the time, effort, and investment well worth the trouble.

Your Results May Vary: Beating the Odds with Submissions

There's an anecdote that has become legend regarding the submission practice of US Poet Laureate Kay Ryan and celebrated poet Jane Hirshfield. Kay Ryan, before she was US Poet Laureate, was teaching at Marin Community College. Both poets lived in Marin County, California. At the start of their careers, they would get together regularly, sit at their kitchen tables, and submit hundreds of packages of poems.

When friends and colleagues got wind of the practice, they asked why they were sending out so many.

"We want to get the editors used to our voices."

Talk about confidence.

Acceptances across the board are 4 percent. That means for every 100 submissions, you will win between two and six acceptances.

I once heard an interview with BEK, a cartoonist with the *New Yorker*. He reported to Terry Gross of NPR's Fresh Air that he mailed a package a week to the *New Yorker*. His work was rejected for ten years. Finally, they published his first cartoon and have been publishing him regularly since.

Back to the Four C's and "firing on all burners": While you are busy writing, you should also be dedicating time to building your writer's resume. This is a challenging aspect of the formula for winning writers. Juggling craft (writing), commitment (submitting), and community (working, often volunteering in the literary community), all while building your confidence, is a tall order.

I know it is. I tried to work the exact program I am recommending to you twice, and failed. I could write, I could revel in kudos, and I could publish—when it was easy. But I could not succeed at all four tasks at once.

A group of poets and I were commenting on the career of a local poet who catapulted from teaching workshops in her home to winning an agent and having her latest collection published by Little, Brown, a major national house. "She works it," everyone agreed. Two of the writers at the table had taken classes with her in her home. She was a good teacher. Her students liked and admired her. "But she was 'out there' all the time—meeting people, schmoozing, hobnobbing." Marion reported. "She wasn't shy, that's for sure," Becky added.

And she stayed the course with her submissions and honing her craft. While her first book didn't impress me, her recent poems in *Poetry* sure did.

One question students often ask is how to submit while you are writing a long piece, such as a nonfiction book or a novel. My answer is that as you are writing a novel, take the time to write a short story and send that around. Or take a short excerpt from the novel, craft it to work like a short story, and submit. Write a review or an article. Keep your name out in the literary world. And, take the time to do at least a small job in the literary community.

When I was a very young writer, I was hanging around in the community of writers and artists in Berkeley. My work was published whenever someone asked. Then I heard that writers were taking the submissions process seriously, going about it in a disciplined, consistent fashion.

Though other writers were engaging in this discipline, it still didn't appeal to me. In the first week of my master's program, a prof pointed down the hall and said, "There's the room with journals. Go look at them and submit." It was never a class requirement, and that was the last word mentioned.

What I learned later (but only after I graduated) was that a key factor in publishing is consistency.

When I became serious about getting published I started a submission practice that went on for over five years. With the help of a submission service called Writer's Relief, I was submitting almost 200 packages of poems or stories per year. In the first year, I had three poems published in the next, six. The numbers went up exponentially in subsequent years. Success breeds success.

Now, I get requests from publishers to send my work. That's a nice change!

How My First Poetry Collection Was Published

On the advice of a friend, I had joined the San Francisco chapter of WNBA. I was working on a novel, but also writing poetry. I had enough poems for a first collection. A friend suggested I self-publish, so I did. I had no plan to sell the books, but I was doing readings.

At a reading, I met a publisher who asked to re-publish my book. That book helped me to cross the divide from "aspiring author" to "published writer." And it paved the way for my second and third books.

Important to note was that, by the time my first book was published, I had been adhering to a regular practice of sending work out. I had twelve poems in my first collection already published. Publishers look closely at your Acknowledgements list when weighing your manuscript against others.

While adhering to a consistent schedule of submissions, there are other ways to get published.

Submitting to journals, print magazines, and online magazines is an excellent way to get started building your writer's resume.

But, as you read above about how *The Long Blue Room* was published, submission opportunities are not always published. Often, you can learn about a magazine looking for new work from friends, or at a conference or Meetup. You can learn about opportunities online, too.

Other ways to keep up your commitment to your submission process:

We've mentioned finding a submission buddy, but, lately, Meetup has groups of writers, online chat groups, and organizations where writers meet. Research where in your community the writers are meeting up.

There's a book titled *The 7 Habits of Highly Effective People.* and the very first habit is to "Be Proactive."

Your life doesn't just "happen." Whether you know it or not, it is carefully designed by you. The choices, after all, are yours. You choose happiness. You choose sadness. You choose decisiveness. You choose ambivalence. You choose success. You choose failure. You choose courage. You choose fear. Just remember that every moment, every situation, provides a new choice. And in doing so, it gives you a perfect opportunity to do things differently to produce more positive results.

"The problem with being a writer is that you always have homework," Jane Ganahl, founder of Litquake, quipped.

Because I had started two successful businesses, I had been trained in the steps necessary to get projects off the ground. Planning. Preparation. Time. And then there's the leap. The leap of faith, the leap of confidence in your project.

A Note on Thinking Outside of the Box

After my first poetry collection was re-published in 2006, I continued to work hard toward my next book. In just a couple of years, I had enough poems for another collection. Over twenty poems of the forty had been published; a respectable amount for the Acknowledgements page, and a good list to catch a discerning editor's eye.

But the second manuscript wasn't getting published as quickly as I expected. I sent it to prizes, contests, and to small presses. One day a lightbulb switched on: I would write to every editor of every journal that had published my work. I was bold, and very direct:

"Thank you so much for being a supporter of my work. I have a manuscript that is looking for a publisher. Do you happen to know any publishers looking for manuscripts?"

As the saying goes "It only takes one." Out of the twenty letters I sent out, one publisher who had been a particularly enthusiastic fan of my work responded; "My writing teacher has a press and I think he'd love your work."

I was elated, when, two months later, Robert Arthur, Publisher of San Francisco Bay Press, accepted *A Dreamer's Guide to Cities and Streams* for publication.

Not only did he accept a manuscript I had been looking to place for over two years, but he also wrote:

"Passages of almost ethereal beauty…lift Joan Gelfand's *A Dreamer's Guide to Cities and Streams* into the realm of the extraordinary. "Transported" alone has more poetry in it than most volumes of contemporary poetry. Here, in a few short lines, we find evocation of the senses, including the sixth, jumped into being by suggestions of beginning, danger, discovery, alarm, assurance, judgement, mission, death and eternity—an archetypal transport to the holy realm of dreaming."

Were those words worth waiting for? I think so!

Since the beginning of this chapter talked about "Prizes, Awards, & Money," why don't we think about a Sample Budget?

How much would you be willing to spend on contests, submissions assistance, contests and prizes?

Sample Budget

How much would you like to dedicate per year to spending on your career?

0.5 or 1% of your salary? Let's say $400–600/year.

Use a submission service twice a year: $200

$200 for twenty contests/award submissions (based on an average cost of $10 per contest)

Willing to go further?

Hire a coach—this can range from $50–300/hour, depending on the coach's track record.

Also, acquire an editor—this can range from $50–150 hour.

–Dos, Don'ts, & a Challenge–

Dos & Don'ts

Do keep up a regular program of submissions.

Do consider dedicating a percentage of your income to your writing career.

Do keep your writer's resume and website up to date!

Don't be intimidated by big name publishers or magazines.

Challenge

Identify your holy grail. Is it writing a book so that you can stand up as the expert on your topic? Is it to win a particular prize? Is it to get a poem in the *New Yorker*, snag a top agent?

Chapter 3

Community

Introduction

It's not what you know, it's who you know.

Have you heard this maxim? Was your first thought, "That's great, but I don't know anyone."

Actually, you do.

But we'll get to that in a minute. If you were fortunate enough to have family (or good friends) in an industry that you wished to pursue, chances are you would have started out with letters of introduction along with movers and shakers' email addresses. Because of "who you knew," you had "access" to a closed and often exclusive community.

While connections are always wonderful, and a personal introduction is often golden, the literary world is an open one which can be accessed by any writer willing to invest the time.

A few years after joining the Women's National Book Association, I was inspired to write up a memo for our membership committee. "Ask not what you can do for WNBA but what WNBA can do for you." The title riffed on John Kennedy's "Ask not what your country can do for you but what you can do for your country." I turned his rhetoric on its head. Remember, good artists copy. Great artists steal.

At the time I wrote the memo, I had met the publisher for "Seeking Center," my first poetry collection, in WNBA. I had been offered numerous speaking and reading opportunities and was getting access to powerful people. I had met Willie Brown, Amy Tan, Michael McClure, Devorah Major, Jack Hirschman, Lawrence Ferlinghetti, Dana Gioia, Molly

Peacock, and numerous other literary icons through readings and events that I had been invited to join, or had had a hand in organizing.

My writer's resume was strong and continuing to grow stronger.

By this time, I had been "promoted" from President of the San Francisco chapter to National Vice President. I presented the memo at a national board meeting in Boston. The meeting included my colleagues from twelve chapters around the country, all of WNBA's committee chairs, and the Executive Committee. They all asked for copies to share my concept with their colleagues.

Here's the memo:

Success Comes from Showing Up

Over the seven years that I've been involved with WNBA, many wonderful and unexpected career-boosting events have occurred. I'm writing this memo not to catalog my personal success, but to encourage us—the leadership—to remind our chapters, and potential members that WNBA is not here only to be served, but to serve. Members, potential and extant, need to see WNBA not only as a "volunteer" organization, but a group of dynamic, highly competent and intelligent women and men who are well connected and willing to help.

While one of our key missions is to fulfill literacy needs for girls and women globally, we are also an important resource for professional development.

Here's a list of WNBA highlights that have happened to me since joining WNBA:

• Became a registered Blogger with the *Huffington Post*.

• "Soccer Mom," a poem, appeared in the international anthology *If Women Ruled the World* published by Inner Ocean Press.

• Interviewed on KPFA radio with California State Poet Laureate Al Young.

• Invited to read at "Art & Soul," a city-wide festival, by a WNBA member.

• Won a spot to read at "Litquake," a prestigious city-wide festival of the literary arts.

• Invited to be on a blogging panel at a Story Circle Network conference in Austin.

• Had "Blogging" article published in Bookwoman.

• Received an invitation to read at Poetry Center San Jose by a fellow WNBA member.

• Had my poetry collection, "Seeking Center," formally reviewed by the President of Poetry Center San Jose.

- Published in PEN/Oakland anthology *Oakland Out Loud*.

- Won an award at the annual Poets Dinner—invited by a WNBA member.

- Won publication in an anthology by an editor I met at Poets dinner.

- Met the founder of Two Bridges Press who published my book, *Seeking Center*.

- Received a glowing endorsement from California State Poet Laureate, Al Young.

- Guest Mentor at California Writer's Club.

- Review, *God of the Jellyfish*, published in Bay Area Poets Seasonal Review (met Poet Lucille Lang Day through WNBA).

The list goes on as far as additional readings I've been offered and connections I've made while being involved with WNBA. So, the next time a potential member hesitates about getting "involved" with WNBA—let them know—ask not what you can do for WNBA, but what WNBA can do for you!

Joan Gelfand
Immediate Past President

The point that I was trying to get across to members (and potential members) was that volunteering is more than just "helping" or "giving" of yourself. If, instead of viewing your volunteer job as a burden, you viewed it as an opportunity, chances are that it very well could produce a positive outcome.

What I wanted to express was that, by volunteering for a literary organization, you would have the opportunity to meet the people you had long admired and, who now were in a position to further your career.

As of this writing, I have been an active member in the Women's National Book Association for over fourteen years. My collaboration with the WNBA has truly been a positive outcome and a "give and take" experience.

While "networking" may have been the hot trend of go-getters and careerists in the late twentieth century, community-building is the sacred ground of the twenty-first century.

Don't get me wrong. There's nothing wrong with "networking." Being transparent that you are attending a meeting or seeking out a particular group to explore what it can offer to you is perfectly acceptable. Direct messages are good; they are powerful and they work.

The good news is that networking was a step up and away from the "old boys' clubs" of the past. It leveled the playing field of "It's not what you know, it's who you know."

Networking gave many women power, opportunity, and a step up.

The Post

The Post is a 2017 movie that tells the story of a moment of truth the press had to face. In the '50s and '60s, the press corps in Washington, DC, was in so tight with the Nixons that the press would not dare to cross them. As a result, truths were withheld from the public about the Vietnam War. The parties, the social gatherings, and the hobnobbing of the press with the White House had blurred the boundaries between the job of the government and the job of the press.

When Katherine Graham decided (against much adversity) to publish the Pentagon Papers, she broke that system apart. The true job of the press was to let the American people know what their elected officials were up to. Graham triumphed as a true leader in the world of serious journalists. Although it was a hard call to go against the White House, it brought back the tradition of muckraking, the journalistic tradition of searching for and exposing real or alleged corruption and scandals.

The closed circles were the power centers of the country. They existed in politics, finance, academia. Networking gave women a chance—a chance to obtain access to formerly closed and hallowed careers, and eventually to financial gain.

Community-building opens the circle even wider. Community-building crosses class, racial, and even experiential boundaries. Instead of the motto, "I'll scratch your back, you scratch mine," community-building is, "I want to help you on your path, even if you never do anything for me."

Community-building means investing time; time to go to meetings and events, time to get to know people. Unlike the myriad of projects that can be completed and checked off at lightning speed—buying airline tickets, making hotel reservations, even getting your laundry picked up and delivered—getting to know people takes time. And in these days of 24/7 jobs, of family and media overload, time has become our most precious commodity.

But the fact remains: Meeting someone once is great; meeting them twice, better. But it's usually not until your third, fourth, and more meetings that you begin to make an impact. It takes time to build a relationship.

I've compiled a list of organizations in the Resources section of the book. Check the membership requirements before you apply. Find the organizations in your home city where writers meet. And don't forget publishers and librarians. They too are a part of the literary landscape and are often the power brokers of a community.

Teresa Le Young Ryan's mantra was "pay it forward." Teresa, a long-time WNBA member (San Francisco Chapter Treasurer), had a philosophy: "What I do now might not benefit me today, but in the future, something good will come of it." The author of *Building your Author's Platform*, Teresa was a cheerleader through and through. She made sure to congratulate all her colleagues on their success, and was always there for questions and to solve problems. When we had WNBA-San Francisco events, Teresa was always there with a camera. Everyone felt included, important, and a part of the community.

Winning writers are supportive, not envious or jealous of other's success.

In my experience, building community is more complex than showing up for a cocktail party, but also more rewarding. Yes, you want to go to that party to see who's looking for a manuscript like the one you have sitting on your computer. But building community also means learning about what interests the people who hold the keys to helping you. Have you read their books? Have you read their client's books? Have you been involved with a cause about which said professional is passionate? In fact, crossing paths with the folks you are building literary community with in other venues always serves you well.

From author Peggy Townsend:

"I knew author Jim Houston as a talented writer and thoughtful teacher. One of my favorite books is still *A Native Son of the Golden West*, which he wrote in 1971. During a talk at the Squaw Valley Community of Writers workshop Jim spoke about landscape as a character. In real life, he said, where we grew up, where we land and where we live shapes who we are. Just like other characters we develop in the books we create, the landscape—an impersonal city, a lonely farm on the plains, a rundown house on the Mississippi—should influence how our characters think and act. Landscape can drive a character and also provide tension. It sets a tone. It should never just be considered background. It's a lesson I've never forgotten."

The Art of Building Community

In some circles, common business practice is to ask for a colleague's card at a cocktail party. The good networker quickly follows up with an email request for an introduction or other professional favor. Sometimes it works out well, sometimes, not so well. Community-building isn't so different, but it does require more time.

Here's an example of a networking experience that didn't end well. Don't worry, I'll follow it up with one that did.

I met a woman at a literary salon who was interested in getting involved with WNBA. She had created an app that was a perfect match for our membership. I saw many wonderful things that WNBA could do to help her get users for the app.

The first time she came to my office, she was over an hour late. After pitching me on her startup, she spent half of our allotted time (I only had an hour) talking about how she had been too busy to date, that her goal was to get the app out, find an agent for her books, and get married.

I had only met her once. I thought she was lovely and personable, but I was on a tight schedule and I didn't have time to counsel her on her personal life. After one meeting, I was not campaigning for the position of friend. I was interested in her as a colleague.

Although I advocated for taking the time to get to know your colleagues, there is a time and a place, right? Some people love to schmooze, they love small talk, and they love gossiping and sharing confidences. Some people prefer to stick to business, are goal-oriented and pressed for time. Know who you are talking to.

While we might not want to think of our "art" or our passion project in terms of anything so crass as selling, the fact is that we writers are selling ourselves all the time. Remember that there are boundaries with professional relationships. Watch for cues that the person you are pursuing is open to a personal connection before you launch in on the history of your dating life!

On the good side, here's a community-building relationship that is truly a match made in heaven: I had the good fortune to meet a woman who asked me to co-host her radio show, invited me to several high-profile readings, helped to get me published in two national anthologies that sold over 50,000 copies, and introduced me to the organizers of an international conference where I've given workshops two years in a row.

I met Kelly Sullivan Walden at a WNBA board meeting in Nashville. She was the President of the Los Angeles chapter and I was the National President. She was a dream scholar. Not a "dreamy scholar," but a scholar of dreams. As an active dreamer and student of dreams myself, we bonded over our common interest.

Did it all happen in the first month? No. I've known Kelly for ten years. And our relationship keeps getting better and more fruitful with each passing year.

Of course, I bought her book, *I Had the Strangest Dream*. It has a permanent place on my nightstand as my "dream bible."

Kelly and I became fast friends. About a year passed by with a few emails. When I found myself in LA, I would invite Kelly to coffee. A short time into our friendship, Kelly invited me to co-host her internet radio show with her. She hosted a weekly show on dreams and asked if I would invite artists and writers who had used their dreams to inform their art. We enjoyed a fruitful and very exciting two years co-hosting her dream show on Awakenings Radio.

I became an advocate of Kelly's. Every chance I had, I told people about her book, and I always included her events and published her news in my newsletter. Our friendship was lovely and reciprocal.

As I got to know Kelly better, I got to know her wonderful, talented, creative, and very open husband, Dana.

Dana had been a songwriter and member of the band Champagne and was fortunate to enjoy a big success in the '70s. As luck would have it, Dana loved poetry!

He particularly loved one of the poems I read on Kelly's show so much that he suggested we make a video of it.

With a lot of work, some expense, and a big commitment of time on Dana's, Kelly's, and my part (we filmed in San Francisco, Santa Cruz and Los Angeles!), that short, unique five-minute video went viral. "The Ferlinghetti School of Poetics" was shown in Athens, Madrid, and at the Beat Museum in San Francisco. Besides receiving over 12,000 hits on YouTube, it has shown at poetry centers and other venues around the country.

Kelly has continued to be an ambassador for my work for over ten years. We've done readings together in Los Angeles, Santa Fe, and San Francisco.

Our recent success expanded our circle even wider: We won a spot to present at the International Association for the Study of Dreams. We taught a workshop on using dreams as inspiration for writing and other art projects. At Kelly's insistence, I entered the short poetry film into the Juried Art show at the dream conference. It was accepted and won a Certificate of Merit.

When Kelly's agent got her the position of co-editor for two anthologies on dreams, Kelly invited me to submit two dreams that she had heard me talk about on the radio show. My essays were accepted in *Chicken Soup for the Soul: Dreams and Premonitions* and *Dreams and the Unexplainable*. Both volumes have sold over 50,000 copies and went on to be Amazon bestsellers.

These wins have been very significant career boosts that helped me along my path. The national publications stand out (as mentioned in Chapter Two on Craft and "building your writer's resume"). Kelly and I have enjoyed a fruitful relationship. The best part is that we truly, truly love each other! There has always been an authenticity to our relationship that grew out of a mutual admiration society. We are ambassadors for each other.

Finding an ambassador is a rare and beautiful thing. When you think you might be finding an ambassador, nurture that relationship. Thank your ambassador and be sure to make yourself available to reciprocate whenever you can.

It doesn't happen for everyone, and there is no science to this, but there is a philosophy that many writers adhere to. It has to do with "paying it forward." Not to sound new age, but, in California, we call it "karma points." In more traditional circles, it is called "doing a good deed."

Going to a reading, buying a writer's new book, and writing a review on Amazon will often make you a friend for life.

Another great example of community-building comes from award-winning poet Andrena Zawinski:

The Women's Poetry Salon: A Model of Success through Community

Writing workshops, academia, conferences, retreats all well serve the craft, commitment, community, and confidence necessary to being a winning writer. Although winning is foremost an internal state, it can also be fostered by being part of a grass roots community of writers that serves to engage and inspire.

The San Francisco Bay Area Women's Poetry Potluck and Salon has been operating as such a community since 2007. Through this model, a diversity of writing voices is connected in a setting in which we feed ourselves every few weeks in private homes with a potluck of food and poetry, celebrating ourselves as women poets through a social extension of our writing as an addition to the regular discipline of studying, workshopping, publishing, promoting, and the business of writing.

We have published a stellar anthology, *Turning a Train of Thought Upside Down* (Scarlet Tanager Books 2012), a collection by forty women poets that has been aptly lauded to reflect the Salon as what it

is: a "garden of voices…from the deep
shared earth of female experience" (Alison
Luterman), voices that "make up an album
of rich fabrics combining the ordinary and
the magnificent" (Grace Cavalieri), voices
that reveal "a range of styles and subjects
approached with honesty and urgency"
(Cecilia Woloch). We maintain a Facebook
page and an email arm for postings on
publications, awards, and readings, and our
gatherings to keep everyone in touch to the
degree to which they wish to participate.

Salonistas, as we have come to call
ourselves, find that to be in a communal
milieu of appreciation and encouragement is
enriching and inspirational as we stir
together a mix of ingredients in a recipe
for being winning writers all."

There really is something to be said for putting yourself out
for other people's interests. A small act of help can signal that
you are not just a self-promoting machine, that you care about
others' careers too.

You just might make more than a fan; you might create
an ambassador.

I met Carol Smallwood through WNBA. She put out a call
for essays on *Women Poets: Writing Editing, Teaching
and Revising.*

I was lucky. She accepted two of my essays.

After that, her interest in me was fantastic. She interviewed me for Bookends. She reviewed my third poetry book. I wrote a review of her book (very acceptable, as we were colleagues).

Last year, I invited her to be the poetry judge for our national writing contest. My national president had someone else in mind, but that writer had never answered my emails, had ignored me on FB, and, although I had asked her directly to include me in her network, she was always too busy. She would have been a fine judge, but I was excited to give my hard-working colleague a break. WNBA's national Contest Judges get tremendous exposure—our ads reach over 100,000 readers, and we receive over 400 submissions.

Out of all of my judges, she was the one who shared the contest flyer almost daily on listservs and worked to spread the word to her professional community. Carol wrote:

```
"I do enjoy working with you as you are
the most ambitious of the women connected
with women groups I've had the pleasure
of working with. So you are my exception.
I send out the contest information on an
average of three every day; I know it takes
so much to get any results."
```

What is the lesson here? Keep your eyes open for that fan who might turn out to be more than a fan. That follow-through is critical when seeking a colleague or ambassador.

Ambassadors are people who include you in their activities, promote your projects, and have exceptionally large networks.

Finding them is like finding gold; it doesn't happen often, but it is a boon when you do!

Here's another story about building community.

A friend and I decided to host a reading at a friend's newly opened wine bar. Since the bar was serving food and wine, we put out a call for poems and writings on "Sexy Food." Through that call for submissions, I met Kit, a woman who ran a popular series. After that reading, Kit invited me to feature at her series. At her series, I met Stephen who hosted a radio show. He invited me to feature—twice—on his radio show. Through Stephen and Kit, I met a large community of Bay Area poets. That one event I organized with a friend was just a fun adventure. I hadn't the least notion that it would lead to doors opening and be a huge career-booster for me. So, when you say, "I don't know anyone"—well, all you really have to do is go out and meet them!

Here are other creative ways that writers have impacted their communities, expanded their networks and created exciting and important work!

Lucy Lang Day was a scientist and a poet. She started Scarlet Tanager Press in 1999 and over nineteen years published sixteen books.

Would Lucy have been as well-known as a poet if she hadn't edited anthologies, collections of dozens of artists and writers?

As an anthology editor, she's opened a door for women from her poetry salon, for Native Americans, and more.

Doing these good works not only gets her name out there, it predisposes other writers and colleagues to like you—you are doing something for the community.

What does all this "good work" translate to? When your book comes out, when you need a review or a favor, all those people that you've helped over the years are there, happily willing to help.

The Story of Jack

I didn't have time to go to many readings or literary events when I was working and raising my daughter, but one Saturday night I headed out with a friend to a PEN event. One our favorite authors, Maxine Hong Kingston, was being featured with a local poet we didn't know.

Maxine was wonderful, but Jack Foley really blew me away. He was personable, brilliant, funny and a very interesting poet. In fact, his work was outstanding, as seen here:

> *I walk the stupid*
> *last mile*
> *into heaven*
> *cursing the light*
> *that blinds me...*
> *I open up*
> *my mouth & hear*
> *a multitude*
> *of voices.*[7]

---

7 Jack Foley, *Technicians of the Sacred* (University of California Press, 2017).

After the performance, I asked for his address. I wasn't exactly sure why, but I wanted to share my work with him.

I sent him a package of poems—poems that I had thought were good but hadn't published. His letters back to me were astounding.

His penmanship was gorgeous, and he took my poems seriously. Our relationship has unfolded over the years. I've been privileged to share a featured reading stage with him twice. What a great feeling to be reading side-by-side with one of my first mentors. We've remained friends and colleagues for over thirty years.

A final case study:

In preparation for this book, I spoke at length with Andrew H. Sullivan, Co-President of C&R Press, along with John Gossee. C&R (meaning Conscious and Responsible) Press was founded eleven years ago by a team of poets. When the press came up for sale, Andrew jumped at the chance, using student loans to procure the press which was set to close. The two writers were already publishing a highly successful international literary magazine, Fjords Review, which focused primarily on poetry and short fiction. The pair was interested in expanding to books and developed a model that would be self-sustaining.

Like many MFA graduates, Andrew knew that creating community was going to be key to a successful literary life.

One of the first clues he got about "It's not what you know but who you know" was a Centerfold map in Vanity Fair. The map drew lines of connection from famous writers to publishers and agents. It outlined how writers met their publishers and agents. It was from reading that article that Andrew realized that networking was going to be key. "'Who you know' clearly made the careers of many famous writers," he told me. His idea for growing C&R press was that taking on the role of publisher himself would place him squarely on the path to meeting the people he wanted, and needed, to know.

As a graduate of the MFA program at Hollins University in Virginia, Andrew was averse to networking and selling himself. He felt the whole "business side" of writing was anathema to his idea of himself as a writer and an artist.

When he realized that the "best way to network was to have a stake in something," he began to enjoy it more. He felt that owning a press was a way to offer opportunities to emerging writers. When he saw his role as a helper, networking became more pleasurable. And, ultimately, he says, he "enjoys being an arbiter of taste."

I hope that by now you see that there are as many ways of building community as there are styles of writing. Put your personal stamp on how you grow your community. Is it finding that ambassador who becomes a lifelong colleague and friend? Meeting someone at an event that you hit it off with and who introduces you to other writers?

Or, do you enjoy hosting events? Celebrating a friend's success? Can you rally writers for events and causes? Try to understand where your passion and strengths are, and you'll find that building community will become second nature.

And then there is building your virtual community.

Social Media Dos and Don'ts

Most savvy publishers have employed social media in their efforts to sell books. A good practice is for the author to be active on social media as well.

But, like craft and building community, there is an art to social media. If you are simply hounding people to buy your book, chances are you won't get substantial results.

Proceed with caution: use social media wisely.

Here's one story: A woman in WNBA had written a book she was hawking—a sort of memoir about growing up with Greek ancestry. I went to her reading because she was a member of WNBA. A few months later she wrote a blog post in answer to a question on Facebook: "What I would tell my younger self."

That post went viral, a publisher found her and the next thing she knew she was being interviewed on radio and TV. And she won a book deal. By not only writing, but being active on social media, her blog post was well-positioned to hit a nerve.

Some publishers and agents these days are advising hopeful authors to put their books online. The idea is that if an author can sell 3,000 (or get 3,000 downloads), it would capture the interest of an agent.

If "buy my book" isn't the most effective strategy, what does work on social media? There are many books on the market about how to use social media effectively. If it is an avenue you would like to pursue, I would recommend you check the references in the back of the book.

For now, here are a few tried and true social media practices:

Remember that social media is also community-building. Virtual community-building, but community-building nonetheless.

Blogs, Twitter, Facebook, all started as a "conversation." The idea was to create a way for people who didn't know each other to connect around topics of mutual interest.

Of course, the fact that the web is open to all also means that there are endless numbers of people joining the conversation. How do you make yourself heard? How do you distinguish yourself as an expert, a writer to follow?

To be a good social media citizen (read that as respected, with a good reputation, don't post self-portraits daily in new outfits or engage in lewd or uncouth behavior), you can leverage social media to help build your reputation. Rule number one is to engage. Find other pages on Twitter, Facebook, LinkedIn, and Instagram who you enjoy following. Respond to comments, articles, retweet, like, and share posts of the people you follow and like. Is there a writer you'd like to know? Find them on FB or Twitter and like their posts. Comment on them and be visible.

Social media marketing may appear random, but it is usually targeted.

I had been using social media as a way to reach friends and as a writer with a series of new books. I had over 3,000 followers on Twitter and about 1,000 on Facebook. When my book *The Long Blue Room* was published, I decided to ratchet up my use of Facebook. I took a friend's recommendation and set up a fan page for the book. After inviting friends and family to like my page, I stalled out at a little under 200. How could this be? I have a personal network of over 1,000 people and over 4,000 people on Twitter and FB.

In frustration, I studied my page. What could I do better? I saw a small icon that said, "Boost this page." Hmm. A small boost would only cost $29. Why not? I was stalled. And, I had been hoping to use social media to boost sales of my book.

When I clicked the acceptance to boost, I was asked to target my audience. I chose as many tags as I was allowed, poetry, literature, all the usual suspects. But I also targeted French readers and France because one poem had won an award in a French journal, and I had once had a very positive experience in France with my work.

Within a week, my page jumped up to over 1,200 likes. That was over 1,000 new potential fans. Okay! I kept my page up with new postings of readings and events, of articles about the book, and any other relevant poetry news.

At the end of the year, when my sales numbers came in from Amazon, I was surprised to learn that I had sold over two hundred copies. After a year, *The Long Blue Room* broke the previous sales records of my other three books. I had employed social media marketing to a positive outcome.

Social media is democratic in a way that in-person interactions are not. You don't have to be a svelte five-foot-eight blonde to garner the attention of fans. (Or a six-foot gym-fit male.) At the same time, you want to "look good" when you build your fan base and connect with people.

When you do launch your Twitter, Facebook, or Instagram page, try not to start out with no friends! Getting a base is easy.

From virtual assistant and social media expert Daniella Granados:

The Dos and Don'ts of Social Media – The Virtual Brain Teaser for Writers

Ah, social media. Posts, follows, and likes. All done with the click of a button and since *everyone* is connected, you'll be able to sell your book fast. Easy enough, no? Well, not so fast. Social media, like anything else, takes time to craft, to produce, and bridges creativity with a side of marketing that can be an enigma for anyone.

I know, I know. You're a writer! Why can't you just write and have that be it? In today's tech-heavy world, one must be able to promote, market, and sell without actually coming across as promoting, marketing or selling.

Today, more people look down at a device than up and around. So, to keep up, here's a few social media dos and don'ts to network like a pro and boost book sales.

Do incorporate a unique branding tool, such as a hashtag, for your book. Use it often and on every social media platform to draw attention. Social media is accessible and free promotion at your fingertips. A hashtag like #YouCanBeAWinningWriter will begin to brand you quickly and effectively.

Don't tell fans and followers outright, "Buy my book!" Instead, give followers something to entice them to buy your book. For example, give them a quick excerpt that ends on a cliffhanger. Then, let them know the rest can be read by clicking on the link. This link will take them to purchase the book!

Do have a plan. Don't wait until the day of to let everyone know you've got a new book listed on Amazon. Instead, space it out and, about a week before the book is available for sale, begin dropping hints of BIG news.

Don't become discouraged if you notice little reaction or few pre-orders. Most buyers will wait until the day of and need reminders of an event happening.

Do reach out to everyone you know. There is no shame in simply informing your friends and family that your book is soon to launch. They are what is called "low-hanging fruit"— those who will support you and help you because they love you. It's a great starting point!

Don't waste time where you are getting no traction. Some campaigns work great on Facebook, others on Twitter—others still on Instagram. It's not an exact science, but focus where you see the most traffic.

Do be patient. Social media takes time to learn. A great rule is to invest some time in learning all of the options available to you (boosting on Facebook, promoting on Twitter, etc.), so you can get the most out of your social media experience and promotion.

Don't do overkill. No one likes someone who seems desperate for a sale. Instead, post excerpts from the book, blog posts, videos or inspiring quotes you like with your purchase link peppered in between. The goal is to draw fans and followers in so they peruse your page, which increases chances of them purchasing.

Do consider your audience. When are people who would potentially be interested in your book connected the most? This is simple demographics. For example, if your book is a young adult fantasy novel, you should post when they are most likely to be online. In this example, readers of YA fiction tend to be online late in the evening. Visibility is key, so considering the schedules of your readers will benefit you greatly.

Don't give up. Most social media campaigns to generate sales fail because most will simply stop posting after the launch date. Or, will ONLY post on the launch date with nothing leading up to it. The formula is easy to remember: frequency over time = sales.

To highlight this example, consider cartoonist Adam Ellis. He posts one to two comics a day and receives thousands of comments and likes. Every three days or so, he will post a link to his funny T-shirt line which is how he makes the bulk of his income. He sells. A lot. Because he is giving readers something for nothing *first*, they are more willing to support him in turn.

Bottom line: Connection is key. Nurture your social media accounts to build a base and the more you water them, the more success you will have. Remember, you CAN be a winning social media pro, too!

The Magic of Coworking

If you are an extrovert, here's the good news: Readings, interviews, and talks are fun propositions.

The bad news? Extroverts generally do not relish the prospect of working alone.

The answer?

Coworking! Coworking grew out of the phenomenon of small startups (three to six people) with sufficient funding for rent but without the need for an entire office space. Coworking spaces offer the best of both worlds: privacy, community, and meeting rooms.

Co-work spaces are a shared space where entrepreneurs, sole proprietors, independent contractors, small startups, and people like you and me work. We work together, but separately. For me, that was just the motivation I needed. I needed both a quiet place to work and to be around the energy of other people working.

Previously, we talked about solitude. By necessity, all writers, even "winning writers," need to have a tolerance for solitude. Fortunately, I was wired for solitude. When I got the chance to work on my writing full-time, I grabbed it.

I found coworking to be the answer to my diminishing productivity. And I fed off the energy of being around other people who were working.

I still have to be organized about my time and careful not to schedule too many meetings with my friends who work nearby.

By having a place to "go" to work, I have days where I know that, if I had stayed home, I would have not been productive. In one year, I finished a book proposal, wrote blog posts, reviews and poems, and finished this book.

The bonus of coworking? Beside the stimulation of working around like-minded people, I had a chance to network with potential readers and clients.

Many years ago, Ethan Canin, then living in San Francisco, started "The Grotto." The idea behind the Grotto was that writers' productivity would increase if they were situated with other writers in a more structured environment. He also felt that the collegiality would decrease the isolation that many writers suffer and that keeps a percentage of writers from embarking on their writing journeys.

The concept was a winner. Journalists and authors work, mingle, and network. The Grotto offers classes and workshops, and also has conference rooms.

The workspace is a place for writers and is still thriving. But the wait list is long. By joining a co-work space, I have everything the Grotto offers, but am mixed in with people working in different fields.

Online Communities

She Writes Press is unique in the world of publishing because it is neither traditional publishing nor self-publishing. SWP gives authors a traditional house experience, complete with an experienced editorial and production team, while allowing them to retain full ownership of their project and earnings. It has been called hybrid publishing, partnership publishing, and co-publishing, and all of these terms are representative of what they do.

Brooke Warner, founder of SheWrites, builds community by not only being the largest online community of women writers, but also offering advice, classes, meetups, and workshops. Writers can sign up for classes online with SheWrites University, sign up for SheWrites camps, and access many other educational offerings.

A writer herself, Ms. Warner sees value in giving women opportunities and flexibility.

I don't have time!

Is social media a waste of time? Listen to these stories:

Diane's Social Media Success

Diane is a writer, musician, and publisher who was following many publishers she liked on Facebook. One was a press in India. When the earthquake hit Tibet, Diane engaged with the Indian publisher, sharing his posts, raising money for relief funds and empathizing with the trauma the country was suffering through. Diane told the Indian publisher about a manuscript that she had created (complete with photos of now destroyed cities and villages) on a visit to Tibet in the 1980s. Her book was a living record of a country that didn't exist anymore.

The publisher's interest was piqued. Diane invited him to teach in San Francisco. They became friends, and when he saw her manuscript he decided to publish it!

A success story—yes!

But that wasn't all. Diane's other success story is that she was following Glass Lyre, a press that she particularly admired.

She and the publisher exchanged comments, and became Facebook friends. When Glass Lyre opened their reading period, Diane submitted her manuscript, "Canon for Bears and Ponderosa Pines." The publisher chose Diane's manuscript.

What a great story. Through reading, sharing, and commenting on sites, Diane had created an authentic connection. By being respectful and earnest, she had succeeded in creating a positive experience with her virtual community.

Come to My Reading

After years of going to friend's readings, attending readings at local bookstores, and inviting my friends and community to my events, I came up with the idea for an app.

It's called cometomyreading.com.

Because reciprocity is so valued in the literary community, the idea is to "gamify" your commitment to attending events. For every event you go to, you get rewarded. You also get to keep track of who is going to which events.

You might not realize it, but we've all been "gamified." Buy groceries, get points. Airlines, hotels, shopping malls, cafes have all subscribed to loyalty programs! Websites like Foursquare and Dodgeball have enjoyed tremendous success.

An idea we are test marketing involves writers in major metropolitan areas. The idea is to place a value on reciprocity; the give and take, paying it forward, and creating community that helps writers to build that critical literary community.

By setting up a reputation system, you are rewarded with badges and stars, and become known as someone who "shows up for others" in your writing community.

All you have to do is go to the Twitter site @cometomyreading. You tweet a picture of the bookstore, event location, and author. You also reference the author's Twitter handle.

On the site, users will see, "Mary Brown went to Louise Parker's reading at Pen is Mighty bookstore." You will also be performing another important task: Supporting your local independent bookstore!

At this writing, pilot programs are active in San Francisco and New York. As the idea grows, we will expand to additional markets.

Building a Fan Base

Part of building a platform is building your fan base. But...how can new writers win fans?

For many of us, the idea of "fans" is a foreign and intimidating concept. Don't worry. Fans doesn't imply screaming teenagers at a concert. What a publisher wants to know when they ask about your platform (and fans) is this: What is the number of people who will reliably buy your books?

These are friends, family, and yes, fans (community) who, when called on, will enthusiastically write a glowing five-star review on Amazon. But, most importantly, these are the folks who will also become a fan of your book and will tell their friends.

Building a fanbase—one fan at a time!

Let's start with your family. Your family will be your first and biggest fans. After all, they were the ones who recognized your talents at the tender age at which you began to display them. They were your sounding board and your first audience when you read them your poems and stories. You tested out your ideas, hypotheses and book concepts on them, right? Now that your book is here, they feel almost as invested in it as you do!

Next steps: Did you write a book review that made the local news when you were in junior high? Edit the school paper? Have a poem published in high school?

These are the folks who believe in you and really *want* you to succeed. If you count, you might realize that you already have more fans than you think.

That said, most publishers require that you have a platform (fan base) before they consider a contract with you. This section gives tips on the hard work you can do to build a fanbase—before you talk to that publisher. Winning writers don't wait to be asked about their platform and fan base—they devote an entire page to the topic in their book proposals.

Think about an Olympic event. Athletes win fans fast because they have talent in their field. That's step one. (Craft!)

These athletes have been vetted over the years by lesser competitions, by judges, by preliminary competitions. They succeeded in high school, then in college. They were in the minors, or local leagues. They have trained and trained and trained.

Now, you're watching them compete on TV. Thousands, maybe millions of people are watching. How did these athletes build their fan base?

1. Deliver what they promised

2. Reliable

3. Professional

Nina Amir, author of *Blog a Book*, discusses building a platform, and one method of tricking yourself into writing a book:

> "Writers need to build a platform if they want to succeed as authors, but, most often, they don't and, sadly they rebel against this task. They just want to write…even though many don't write consistently.
>
> Bloggers, on the other hand, write consistently and develop platform as part of the 'job.' And those who succeed at attracting a large audience sometimes land book deals or successfully self-publish because they have a built-in readership for their books.
>
> And that's why aspiring authors benefit from using a blog to write their books and build platform at the same time.
>
> The world of blogging changes rapidly, but it remains one of the most efficient ways to share your work with an eager audience. In fact, you can purposefully hone your blog

content into a uniquely positioned book—
one that agents and publishers will want
to acquire or that you can self-publish
successfully.

You do this by writing and publishing a
saleable book based on a blog. Develop
targeted blog content that increases your
chances of attracting a publisher and
maximizing your visibility and authority as
an author.

Whether you're a seasoned blogger or have
never blogged before, blogging a book offers
a fun, effective way to write, publish, and
promote your book, one post at a time."

This method has proved successful for many authors. It is not unlike setting a timer, writing for an hour a day, except that is serving two functions: Not only are you getting your writing for the day finished, but you are also building a network, a platform, and a fan base at the same time.

Word of Mouth

People talk.

From the American Marketing Association:

"Harnessing the power of word of mouth,
both in social media and face-to-face, may
call for turning to some of the basics of
media. It's not just who the audience is for
your marketing message, but how different

members of your target audience participate in receiving and passing along information about brands. How do traditional and social media interact with each other to create some type of in-market impact? For example, do social media amplify the effect of traditional media or do they have their own distinct impact, or both?

To achieve the potential of social media, marketers will have to understand better how it works in concert with offline word of mouth. The new research that is being conducted suggests that there are answers to this challenge, but they are not simple. It may require systematic processes for applying the learning from social networks to creative message and media development, analogous to what marketers have done historically with traditional media, to determine what works, and what does not."

Word of mouth is the recommendation of one friend to the next.

"I loved this book! I think you will really enjoy it too." Recommendations from friends and associates whom you trust is a seal of approval; you can rest assured that you won't be wasting your time and money.

Beyond Fans

Platforms: What are They and Why Do I Need One?

Among the many questions that agents and publishers ask a new author is, "What is your platform?"

Platform is a common industry term. What the agent or publisher wants to know is something really important—how many books are you really going to sell?

Because, while every author dreams, imagines, and hopes that *everyone* in the world wants to buy their book, an agent or publisher wants you to prove to him or her that at least 3,000 people beside your friends and family *will* in fact buy your book.

How does someone who has been "just writing" create a platform?

Here's an extreme example. Michelle and Barack Obama's lucrative book deal.

> "His is going to be easily the most valuable presidential memoir ever," said Raphael Sagalyn of the ICM/Sagalyn Literary Agency, who predicted that Mr. Obama could earn as much as $30 million with a two- or three-book contract. "And I think Michelle Obama has the opportunity to sell the most valuable first lady memoir in history."

The fact that Barack and Michelle Obama presided over the everyday events of the most powerful country in the world certainly earned them fans, and, now, readers.

The world is their platform. While others of us are not so fortunate, here are some ideas for how you can describe your platform in your book proposal, and also for how to build your platform.

Although it helps, you don't have to be Keith Richards, Richard Simmons, or Michelle Obama!

- You teach at a university

- You are involved with your alumni/college/grad school

- You are active in a club

- You are a member of professional clubs

- You volunteer at (symphony, local food banks, etc.)

- You are employed by a large corporation that supports the outside activities of employees

- You are on a board

- You are active in your child's school/league

- You have a column in a local paper

- You have a website with large numbers of followers

- You have a significant following on YouTube, Twitter, Facebook, Instagram

While some of these might be out of reach, others can be accomplished in a short period of time. Other "platforms" can take years to build. Winning writers are busy building their platforms as they are writing their books.

Joining an organization is one thing. Creating relationships with people who will buy your books is another. Let's go back to "investing" in your career.

How much time are you willing to invest?

Being active in the public arena by volunteering, starting a reading series, even just going to readings, will show people that you are serious about being a part of the literary community. These are the people who will become your readers, and your platform.

Bay Area author Beth Lisick met the editor of *Best American Poetry* when she read at an open mic. She had no book, no fan club. According to Beth, she had nothing beside a stack of poems. That editor liked her work well enough to invite her to publish in *Best American Poetry*. At a celebration for the book, she met an agent who asked if she had a book idea. Thus, Beth Lisick became a winning writer.

While online connections are great and, most importantly, have the capacity to increase your reach to global proportions, there is an undeniable magic that happens when people who share similar interests get together.

Here's a simple story—it can happen to you. Remember the story I told about hosting a reading at a friend's new wine bar? And remember how I met Kit, the woman who ran a popular series and who introduced me to Stephen Kopel, a radio show host? Well, there's one more part of how Kit helped me to build community.

Kit and I both shared a love of home cooking and excellent wine. One night, she invited me to her house for dinner. At the dinner was Jane, a British woman who had recently located to New York.

Jane had started a press and was hosting a reading series in New York City. I submitted to the press's anthologies and was published twice. Every time Jane came to San Francisco, she would invite me to read. I've read for Jane in New York, in Santa Cruz, and in San Francisco. I've invited her to be on the faculty of a writing conference. Just another great example of building community.

Building Community on Your Book Tour

Your first book will help to build your fan base.

When giving readings, visiting new communities and cities, speaking on the radio, or giving interviews, winning writers make sure to capture names and emails of people who attend their events. Everyone from the event coordinator, to your interviewer, to attendees might have an interest in staying in touch.

Tip: Always bring a pad to pass around to capture people's emails. After the event, write to your attendees and ask their permission to be added to your list.

Be on the lookout for future invitations; countless authors report that, after one event, they have received invitations from audience members for future events.

And always remember to follow up with a thank-you note to your hosts!

The Power of YES

Did you ever hear the story of how John Lennon fell in love with Yoko Ono?

Lennon was visiting an art gallery—he considered himself a sketch artist and had gone to art school. There was Ono installing her show. She was installing a huge sculpture, the word YES.

There is a children's book called *Richard Scarry's Please and Thank You*. The book is an object lesson in teaching children the consequences of their actions.

There is a group of characters—Lowly Worm, Pig Will and Pig Won't.

Pig Will does what's asked of him. And, lo and behold, guess what? Pig Will gets the goodies. He gets to participate, have fun, and be an all-around happy guy.

Pig won't, of course, always says no. And, well, you guessed it. Pig Won't doesn't get the goodies.

Simple as this sounds, there is power in taking on the persona of Pig Will.

When people see that you help out, not only are you building your reputation, but you are also doing what we spoke of before: You are "paying it forward."

We know that not all actions are followed by fabulously positive outcomes. But haven't you found that taking positive action—on balance—has benefited you in some way?

The Big, Scary "Yes"

In 2004, I had been on my own for four years. I had quit my corporate job to write my book, had a setback, and was just starting to establish myself as a poet. As with many writers, I was busy! I still had a daughter at home, I was running a small business, and my writing projects had projects.

When a writer friend told me about WNBA, I was thrilled to meet colleagues and friends who were doing what I was doing! Soon after joining WNBA, we members received an email. The current president was stepping down and, if someone didn't take the reins, the chapter would fold. Wow. Okay. I was new to the group, but with the support of another member, we decided to take on the presidency together. Boy, did I get an education. I learned how to plan events, communicate to a group, and get things going. Together, we doubled the members!

Two years later, I was asked to be the incoming National President's Vice President. Now, that was a serious ask. It meant two years as VP, two years as President, and two years as immediate past President. I was really loath to take on a new commitment. I really wanted to get back to my novel. My husband strongly advised that I take on the position.

Since that time, I've had five more books published, two of which were directly related to my leadership role in WNBA. The other three certainly took into account that I had a national platform.

The point here is not about happy endings. In fact, it's the opposite.

The point is that it is often just when you are feeling stretched thin, crunched for time, and really not in the mood that these opportunities to say YES! present themselves.

What I want to say is that it isn't always so obvious when the right time is to say yes. And that building your platform is not exactly like party planning.

Sometimes you say yes exactly when you would be inclined to say NO!

Sometimes you make that extra effort to build your platform at exactly the time when you want to pull in your oars, hibernate, isolate and.... WRITE!

But winning writers, remember, are firing on all burners. Winning writers are building community, working on craft, staying committed, and moving forward with confidence.

A note on teams: Remember that you don't always have to go it alone. When I took on the Presidency of WNBA, I had mentors. Past presidents, executive board members, and chapter members were all sources of great inspiration and encouragement for me.

Loneliness & the Writing Life

"If you are good you will be lonely."

—Mark Twain

"Artists are particularly likely to experience loneliness (existential loneliness). They regularly ask the question: 'Is life worth living?' " Eric Maisel, PhD and author of *Staying Sane in the Arts* says. "One moment the artist feels connected to others, to his god, his ancestors, his descendants. He contemplates human happiness...then in the very next second, he/she finds herself utterly alone...this existential aloneness should not be confused with loneliness. Loneliness can be ameliorated by human contact. Aloneness is a problem that translates roughly to 'life is meaningless' and 'I do not matter.' Aloneness is experienced by the artist as a terrible lack—a chilling lack of purpose.... It can strike in the blink of an eye."

From J. Franzen's book *On Solitude*:

> "Readers and writers are united in their need for solitude, in their pursuit of substance in a time of ever-increasing evanescence: in their reach inward, via print, for a way out of loneliness."

Try to tease apart the feelings when, and if, you do begin to feel "lonely" or "alone." Breaks are also good, even while working on a long, complicated project. Take a break to gain perspective on your project, refresh yourself intellectually and spiritually, and have fun with friends, family, and loved ones. Remember, writing is a solo endeavor. You are there because you chose it!

Challenges

1. Join one new organization.

2. Set a goal of finding an ambassador.

3. Write one nice note to another author or a letter to the editor.

4. Build your fan base: Collect business cards, create an email list, start social media.

Chapter 4

Confidence

"Do not judge me by my successes. Judge me by how many times I failed and got up again."

—Nelson Mandela

Introduction

Doubt can topple the most winning writer.

Full transparency: Lack of confidence almost ruined my chances for a writing career.

> *"What can ruin a first-rate writer? Booze, pot, too much sex, too much failure in one's private life, too much attrition, too much recognition, too little recognition, frustration. Nearly everything in the scheme of things works to dull a first-rate talent. But the worst possible is cowardice."*
>
> —Norman Mailer

I've already told you the story of the Pulitzer Prize-winning novelist editor who summarily broke my confidence in my first book. Truth be told, I was a party to the disaster; after working on that first book on and off for several years, I enthusiastically embraced the editor's suggestion to move on to a new project. With a new project, I'd have a fresh start. It would be better, easier, smoother, right?

Not. And one reason was that I hadn't confronted my confidence issues. Here's what happened with my second novel.

After an excited start, I worked hard with a new editor for three years. After many revisions, meetings and "hard thinks" about plot and character, my editor pronounced the book finished. I should have felt blessed, elated! Except that I wasn't convinced. My editor assured (and reassured) me that this new manuscript was in good enough shape to send out to agents. She really liked the book. She made a point of telling me that she had been editing her husband's book, and after eight years, it still wasn't ready. Mine was ready.

At my editor's recommendation, I sent the manuscript to about six high-powered New York literary agents. Their responses ranged from "It's not for us" to "This is great but not for us." Bottom line: I had no agent.

After crying and self-flagellation for sending it out too soon, I found solace only in hours on long, solitary walks. I had to sort out my frustration and disappointment. After some months, I decided that I couldn't just let this book die. I had already done that with one book, right? I steeled myself and researched another group of agents.

I sent it out on my own to about ten agents. When one agent responded that he liked the book, but asked if I had I ever published fiction before, I took his inquiry as a rejection. I never answered him and stopped sending the book out.

Another factor working against me was sociological. When I began writing the book, the world was flush in the midst of Silicon Valley's 1999 tech bubble. Massive numbers of workers under the age of thirty had become fabulously wealthy. Interest in Silicon Valley goings-on was at a fever pitch. When I sent my book out in 2002, the bubble had burst. New York agents were smirking; tech was so over.

As the saying goes: timing is everything.

Sometimes the lack of interest in your project by editors and publishers is not about your writing, or your book. Sometimes a lesser book strikes a zeitgeist; sometimes your timing, and your topic, is off. That said, there is still a chance that you can locate your niche. Seek out groups on social media with an interest in your topic. Research organizations with an interest in your topic.

My crisis of confidence cost me months of productive writing time. And it cost me years of not getting my first novel out.

That Silicon Valley novel sat in the drawer for seven years! It haunted me. As I went about my life, I felt like I had abandoned ship; that I had left something for dead that was still breathing. I knew the book was good; I believed in my characters, and I believed that I had a story to tell about women in the tech workplace, about America and class differences.

When the tech world took a turn in 2009, when the economy rebounded, when Silicon Valley was sexy again, I pulled the book out. I still loved it.

As I was looking for a publisher for the novel, I found a publisher for my third poetry manuscript that I had been working to place. I turned my attention away from the novel toward the new book of poetry. It was a bird-in-the-hand moment.

Soon after the poetry book came out, a friend of my husband's relocated to the Bay Area. After living on the east coast, he had just started a publishing company and was especially interested in transmedia projects. Within a month, he bought my Silicon Valley novel!

We worked together for a year, revising the book and preparing for publication. Then, in an unexpected turn of events, the publishing company, Encanto Press, changed their company strategy to only handle screenwriters. All rights reverted to me. I didn't take this unfortunate turn personally. It was a setback, but I still felt good about the book. And, best of all, having won a book deal had given me back my confidence.

It took another year, but I found my publisher. In fact, I found two.

Clearly, this is a story of commitment as much as confidence. If commitment and confidence are so intertwined, how do we tease them apart?

Here are some exercises that might help.

1. Do you ever dream that the book you finished but put aside is being published?

2. Do you find yourself thinking about your book—its unfinished passages, its pages that you still wish you could polish?

3. Do you find yourself angry or frustrated when a colleague, friend, or stranger publishes a book that is on your topic, or on a similar theme as the book you abandoned?

If you answered yes to any of the above questions, I would recommend that you take the time to revisit the book. Take it out and look at it with fresh eyes. See if it still works for you. Show it to someone new who hasn't seen it before.

If you answered yes to any of the above questions, I would venture to say that your unpublished book has more to do with your confidence than with your commitment.

Another idea is to talk to people who were fans of your book in the beginning—the early readers who read your book before it was rejected by agents and criticized by editors.

To boost my confidence, I read biographies of people who faced insurmountable challenges including Steve Jobs, Winston Churchill, and Ray Charles. Then there were women writers like Isabel Allende (who survived a political coup which killed her father during the reign of Pinochet). Allende was forced to flee her native country and live in exile. As if that wasn't debilitating enough, Allende also lost her daughter, whom she memorialized in the memoir "Paula."

Jeanette Walls, author of *The Glass Castle*, survived abuse, an alcoholic father, and extreme poverty, as did Dorothy Allison, author of *Bastard Out of Carolina*.

Other authors who overcame terrible odds were Toni Morrison, Janet Frame, and even the French author Colette, who lived through World War two in Nazi-occupied Paris.

"You gain strength, courage, and confidence by every experience in which you really stop to look fear in the face."

—Eleanor Roosevelt

Check my narrative arc against how National Medal of Honor-winning writer Joan Didion found her groove:

In the documentary *The Center Will Not Hold*, Joan's mother recognized how much Joan enjoyed writing. She saw a writing contest advertised in Vogue magazine. "You could win this contest," her mother suggested. Joan entered and she won! That contest gifted the winner with a job at Vogue in New York. Joan Didion's career was launched.

Pretty cool, huh?

Joan Didion went on to publish articles about the sixties, novels, and screenplays. Mid-career, she become impassioned about the war in El Salvador. She wanted to write about the war, but she didn't believe that she had what it takes to be a war correspondent.

But her editor believed in her, and not only encouraged her, he sent her to El Salvador to write. Her first press trip resulted in a book-length essay called "Salvador" and cemented Didion's place as a writer on political and social issues.

Heeding the Call

What If Being a Winning Writer Could Save Your Life?

Moira—Greek origin—"a person's fate, destiny"

In 2012, a friend of mine had an idea for a book. Caroline had been a Fulbright scholar, spoke Italian and Spanish fluently, and had spent her career as a reading specialist.

She loved children and raised her own child to be a citizen of the world.

She also loved food. She baked the best biscotti you've ever eaten. A slight woman, she nevertheless devoured recipes, read books about food, cooked with her husband in the kitchen, entertained beautifully, had a gorgeous home, and even spent summer afternoons canning fruit and tomatoes with her daughter.

Her Italian soups, salads, and vegetable dishes were perfectly composed and tasty creations that her guests raved over. She often signed up to listen to cookbook authors speak about their craft and their views on food. She would become enthusiastic and passionate about new chefs and restaurants. A world traveler, she took cooking classes in Vietnam, Thailand, Italy, and other exotic locales.

When she retired, she had a passion to publish a book for babies. The book was to be a series of photos of foods paired with the names. Blueberry. Picture of blueberries. Simple.

She did one mockup. She had ideas for other books, too.

I gave her a list of tasks to think about to help get her book projects off the ground: "Join the Society of Children's Book Writers & Illustrators immediately. Join the Women's National Book Association," I advised early on. I even gave her the names of a few agents that I knew who were interested in children's books.

She ignored my advice. She sent the book to one or two publishers. The book was rejected. I advised her to keep going. I gave her encouragement. I offered to help her with her book proposal.

She dropped the project like a hot potato.

I was discouraged, not because she hadn't hired me as a coach or taken my advice, but because I thought the aesthetic and philosophy behind her book made it a beautiful and worthy project. I thought that, in combining her passions for food and reading, she had hit on something that was unusual and valuable.

A while later, she asked me for my astrologer's name and contact information.

She told me that she had spoken with Deborah, but didn't tell me much about the conversation and I didn't pry.

Fast forward five years. After experiencing shortness of breath, Caroline learns that she has a very rare sarcoma. When I see her two months after her diagnosis, she looks wan, and worried.

The next day, I send her a note. I'd like to come by to do some *reiki* on you. My feeling with reiki is that, since I got my transmission from a reiki master, I always try to visit friends and family who are ill and do the reiki on them. It is not a business, it is a love offering.

After I offer to come by and reiki her, she answers me with a heartfelt email in which she confesses that my astrologer had told her "If you don't publish your children's books, you will die."

This is her exact email:

> *Ok, this is going to sound strange, but here goes. Remember when you gave me your contact Deborah for astrological charts? I didn't pay any attention when she said if I don't publish my children's books I would die. Well I didn't publish my books and here I am at death's door. My question to you is: can I publish them online?*

I had to think for a minute. Her email had caught me off guard.

"ASAP? Is that possible? I believe in all this. If you can help me set up online to publish it might just save my life! What do you think?"

I wrote her back, suggesting that she look up Amazon's Create Space.

A short time before I learned that my friend had cancer, I had hosted a literary salon and invited my colleagues from WNBA to listen to two WNBA authors who had just published new books, both passion projects.

One was a memoir of living in Paris as an expat during the '70s, and the other was a survey of gay and lesbian heroes and heroines.

The author of the Paris memoir had had a roller-coaster of a ride. A successful nonfiction writer and expert on Gertrude Stein, not only had her manuscript been rejected by publishers with whom she had introductions and connections, but she had also worked with a publisher who gave her a contract and then "pivoted"—changed his business.

Finally, she made a connection with a publisher. The publisher was small, and didn't really do the right things to sell her book. She hired a publicist, but she didn't really deliver except for a couple of readings and one review.

When she was disappointed in her sales numbers, I reminded her—you had to write this book. Some books are not written for the bestseller lists. They are written for love.

Nine months after the publication, the book was nominated for a prestigious literary award. The award inspired new interest and gave my friend hope that, even if her numbers hadn't been what she had hoped for in the first months, the story wasn't over yet.

Elaine Bond: A Children's Book Author Started Small, Ended Big!

Elaine had good credentials; she had been a science writer with the University of California, Berkeley. She left her job to create photography books. She started with a small book, *Affinals*, that "shares wisdom from forty wild animals, from the snow leopard to the honeybee to the frillfin goby (a small jumping fish). Their affirmations come alive through beautiful illustrations and heartening, well-researched tales of the wild."

From there, she began to be recognized for her photography. Her next book was with a university press and the next two with a popular, nationally distributed small press.

One day, at a salon, Elaine held up her new book. I gasped (to myself). Elaine had created a book for babies that was just Susan's idea. And she had a publisher.

And there you have it.

From Kelly Sullivan Walden, the author of nine books on heeding the call:

A woman has the dream that she is in a bar and a woman approaches her with a drink and as the woman gets close to her, she throws the drink in her face, hits her over the head with a glass and yells in her face, "Wake up."

And the woman wakes up from her dream and she's covered in water and she's got a bump on her head and she's holding a glass. And she realizes that she did this to herself. She poured water on herself, hit herself on the head and was yelling the words "wake up."

And she sat on the edge of her bed drenched

and aching and saying, "What am I supposed to be waking up to?" So, she sat down to write. She started journaling and she realized as she was journaling for the first time in years. What came through her journaling was, "You're a creative—" what's her—"a masters in MFA in Creative Writing and you teach creative writing in X, Y and Z schools and you are constantly encouraging your students to write and yet you have not written creatively in years. You must write."

So, she continued her journaling and it turned into pages and pages and pages of a story, of a fictional story that turned into poetry and cut to present time. She's changed her life. She's no longer teaching, she's writing full-time and making a living at it. And she's living in Mexico, she's traveling all over the place and she's got a totally different life—unrecognizable from the life that she had at that time.

And some of the background of what was happening at that time in her life was that her house which was—she had put all of the money that she had made and saved into this "dream house" that was completely falling apart and causing so much stress. And she ends this story by saying, "Instead of plunking all my money down into my dream house, I thought I would just put my money and energy into living my dreams instead."

Renate: Interview with Renate Stendhal, PhD

Renate is an award-winning writer who has had a fascinating and circuitous journey. Raised in Germany, she is now an author and renowned art and culture critic for the international publication *Scene 4*.

Renate started her writing career as a culture correspondent for German media while she was living in Paris. Her pieces were aired on radio and published in magazines. She translated Gertrude Stein's only mystery novel, *Blood on the Dining-Room Floor*, into German, and in 1989 created a photo-biography with parallel visual and textual readings of Stein's life, titled *Gertrude Stein: In Words and Pictures*. The English edition (Algonquin Books, 1994) earned a Lambda Award. In 2009, the photo-biography was published and served as an inspiration for dual art exhibitions: "Seeing Gertrude Stein: Five Stories," Summer 2011, at the Contemporary Jewish Museum of San Francisco, and at the National Portrait Gallery in Washington, DC. Renate was involved in the educational programming surrounding the show and the parallel exhibition "The Steins Collect: Matisse, Picasso and the Parisian Avant-Garde" at SFMOMA. Her blog, quotinggertrudestein.com, followed the preparations, the "Summer of Stein," and the aftermath of the epochal exhibitions.

Of interest for writers is that the Gertrude Stein exhibitions were held fifteen years after the publication of Stendhal's *Gertrude Stein in Words and Pictures*. The exhibits imbued Ms. Stendhal's book with new readers, new sales, and a new life.

In the '90s, Stendhal pursued degrees in psychology, studying a particular school of intuitive listening. As a writer, a reviewer, and a psychologist, I was very much interested in Ms. Stendhal's views on confidence and the writing life.

In two lengthy interviews, we discussed the arc of her career and what advice she could give to writers, given all that she had experienced.

My first question to Renate was: "Why do you think that writers suffer the all-too-common crisis of confidence?"

"With writing, and with most arts, the inner critic takes over. When a writer's confidence falters, it is as if a censor has taken up residence on your shoulders whispering: "What horseshit! Stupid sentence!"

"If you hear enough from your inner critic, you give up. Even if others, your best friend or your partner, tells you that your piece is good, you don't believe it." She continued, "It is important to know *who* is speaking. Is it your mother, your father, your first lover? An unsupportive teacher?"

In Renate's case, it was her fifth-grade German teacher who discouraged her from writing.

Stendhal was a prolific young writer who, by the age of eight, had already hand-scribbled some one hundred pages of a novel. Also, she was writing poems.

"I want to see everything! Everything and never be opposed," she wrote in a poem at age six.

Her teacher was incredulous: "Who is helping you?"

When Renate offered the rejoinder that these were in fact her own words, her teacher chastised her: "Don't lie to me!"

This went so far that her mother made a visit to the school. After the parental visit, this unsupportive teacher now at least believed that her student was in fact responsible for the writing. The teacher didn't mince words: "I don't care for it at all," she told Renate's mother. "It is overwritten."

Her mother returned home and advised her to "tone it down."

According to Stendhal, the whole episode "doomed" her. She lost her footing. What to tone down? Her love of the world? Her love of writing? "What a disaster," Renate reported. "My joy of writing got a leak in the boat."

But writing would not let her go. As a teenager, she decided to write serious poetry. This time, her nemesis and detractor showed up in the form of a boyfriend. "Frantisek was already accomplished. He was reading Andre Gide and Sartre—existentialists. He was a gifted writer." Four years her senior, her boyfriend called her "my little poetess." He said not a word about her first poems and advised: "Write another one hundred. Then we will see."

"When we became lovers," Stendhal explains, "we were soon competing. One day he said, 'I have a hard time writing when you are in the next room writing—couldn't you do something else?' "

"So, I dropped out of literature studies and went into ballet—to get out of my head."

Soon after, she traveled to Paris alone to study dance. There, she eventually did underground theater and became a journalist. "You pick up a thread wherever you can. If it is your destiny, you go. For me it was writing, so I put my energy into journalism."

What else would Ms. Stendhal like to say about confidence?

"You have to have experience in order to have confidence."

"I wrote. Anything! Ad copy, articles. I translated Susan Griffin, Adrienne Rich, and Audre Lorde. I was learning by doing."

Stendhal found herself in the right place at the right time. "Feminism came and told women that we had a voice. I could take my stories, my hidden treasures, and take them into the world." And, she added, "Confidence builds." It was around this time of her life that she got a fabulous break.

"Two lesbian women took over a publisher in Germany. I went to meet them and said that I wanted to translate something for them. 'Take your pick among our authors,' they replied. I picked Gertrude Stein and translated her one and only detective novel. Then I pitched creating a photo biography, *Gertrude Stein in Words and Pictures*. They said yes."

That success helped Renate over the hurdle of fighting with her inner critic every day—every moment! "I have to be like a child in a sandbox, instead of being so serious about every word a so perfectionist. I suggest: Dare to be a fool—write an idiotic sentence and let it be. Look at it—then look deeper. Is there another sentence there? I give myself permission to be an idiot."

David Gaughran, author and marketing guru, put it best:

"There is a necessary dichotomy in every writer's brain: We need a certain level of self-belief to put our work out into the world, but also a healthy dose of self-criticism to ensure its quality.

Dealing with this dichotomy is the biggest writing challenge I've faced. And it's one I still face, every single time I sit down to write.

The solution (like the problem) is in your own head. You don't need that critical voice when writing the first draft. In fact, you should ignore it, because it can make you freeze up completely. If you start being critical about your opening page, you'll never finish that first chapter, let alone the book.

You need to vomit up the words until you hit The End.

Then you can be critical.

Everything can be fixed in the second draft... except for a blank page.

Give yourself the freedom to get the bones of your story down on the first pass.

You can worry about putting flesh on those bones later. Because once you have that first draft done, nothing can stop you."

Second Guessing: Avoiding the Sand Trap

An article in a writer's magazine a few years back described the difference between male and female authors. The article was a wakeup call, shedding a harsh light on the ways in which women's inner critics keep them from succeeding.

In her well-researched article, the journalist had interviewed many magazine editors.

The overall finding was dismal. "When we write a letter to an author, rejecting the work they sent us but letting them know that we liked their work and inviting them to submit to us again, overwhelmingly, the men send us new work. The women, we never hear from again. They take our note as a rejection."

The verdict seems to be that women have a tendency to second guess their decisions. Do you?

I hope this story helps any of you who are having a crisis of confidence about the depth and interest of your characters, and your own abilities.

"Weird Little Super-Powered Heart" by Tanya Egan Gibson

One evening, I confessed my deepest fear to Stephanie Moore, whose writing workshops I attended: My characters weren't "sophisticated" the way characters in literary fiction all seemed to be. They had "big round baby feelings" the way I, in fact, had big round baby feelings, and I was positive that people would laugh at them. At me. People would laugh at me! Nobody intelligent could have such dumb, sappy, unsophisticated feelings! My characters had weird little hearts because I had a weird little heart. And I couldn't seem to be able to write my way around this. I couldn't change it.

"Don't change it," Stephanie told me. "It's going to set you apart." She said she and the other writers in the workshop loved it—and me—because we were different. "You should write that phrase down," she added, "'big round baby feelings'—and put it in your book."

For over fifteen years now—through Stephanie's passing away, through those other writers becoming some of my closest friends, and through that novel, How to Buy a Love of Reading, being published (with "big round baby feelings" indeed making its way into the text)—I've shared this advice with my own students and with clients for whom I edit. Whatever you fear makes you different is, in fact, your writing superpower, and the more you embrace it, the stronger your writing becomes."

Meet the Team: Your Publicist and Coach

How Working with Publicists and Coaches Can Increase Your Confidence

When I was launching my second poetry book, I had the good fortune to hire a publicist at a price I could afford. Kim was a WNBA member who loved poetry and had connections throughout the country.

My first poetry collection, *Seeking Center*, had been well received, but I had done nothing to set up readings, get the book reviewed, or even hawk it to bookstores. Writing was one thing; promoting myself was a task that I was unskilled in and for which I was woefully unprepared.

Needless to say, that first book didn't sell especially well.

For my second collection, *A Dreamer's Guide to Cities and Streams*, Kim worked tirelessly on my behalf. She set up readings, helped me put together a press package, got my galleys out for reviews and interfaced on important business (like getting the book up on Amazon and sending the book out for post publication awards) with my publisher.

She challenged me to think hard about my identity as a writer. Who was I speaking to and why? What was my niche? My angle? My position and/or artist statement?

It was with Kim's help that I realized that many of my most loved (and frequently published) poems were eco-warrior-, social-justice-, and politically-oriented. She confidently labeled me an "activist" poet, something I would never have had the confidence to do on my own.

What Kim was doing was simple; she was leveraging the success I had had with publishing political poems. She used a note about my poem "War Rant," in which a magazine editor wrote: "I have just watched a documentary on the BBC about John Lennon and I remembered how artists can be the social conscience. Then I saw "War Rant" and put it atop the New Verse News," in my press release. When I got the note, I was flattered, but I was clueless about what it implied in the bigger picture of developing an identity for myself.

Other poems had also gotten a lot of play and recognition from publishers, in particular "Requiem for a Dying Planet," Russian River Watershed," and "Ghazal for Baiji."

It was only by working with Kim, a seasoned book marketer and publicist, that I began to grow more confident in myself as part of a community of socially responsible writers and artists. Having the support of a professional who believed in my work helped bring me into a new phase of being a public figure.

Other Writers on Working with Publicists

It was Hillary Clinton who popularized the term, "It takes a village." I've always found that phrase so supportive. When I was a single working mother, when I've been up to my eyeballs with projects, and at other stressful times in my life, I just take a moment to remember, "It takes a village."

When it comes to your book and getting the word out about it to the public, it most definitely takes a village.

Many tasks are manageable; social media, writing a monthly newsletter, and keeping your fans informed about your speaking engagements, for instance.

But nothing beats a third-party referral. And some festival organizers, bookstore events managers, and university event planners have a policy of not speaking to writers directly.

To that end, having a team to negotiate event details is invaluable. Most importantly, your team will be able to introduce you to event organizers with whom they have established relationships.

How to hire a publicist

Book publicists' fees vary widely. I've worked with a publicist for as little as $500 month and have heard of fees as steep as $3,000.

When choosing a publicist, you will want to know the breadth of the "Rolodex"—the contacts and database of the company, the track record of sales, and the willingness to promote your book. Are they helping you with a press release? Press kits? Do they have a list of publications that will consider reviewing galleys? Do they have connections with decision makers in your field?

As loath as you might be to invest yet again more of your own funds (especially after hiring an editor and/or a coach), this is a step that can make or break the success of your book.

A good publicist can set up TV and radio interviews, get your book well-placed in a library or bookstore, and can even help you organize a campaign to be a bestseller!

Most publicists have the knowledge of what it takes to become an Amazon or *NYT* bestseller.

Note: The success and sales of each subsequent book that you publish impacts the size, resources, and support that you will receive from your next publisher.

Coaches: How to Maximize the Bang for Your Buck

As with publicists, writing, career, and life coaches can be credentialed. They all should have developed track records that you can easily check. Do current and past students and clients recommend them? Have they offered to make connections for you? Are they empathic or tough love? Does their style match your needs?

I didn't know that I needed a coach until I met Judy. Judy had worked with artists for many years including writers Michael Crichton and Marc Norman, the co-author of *Shakespeare in Love*. Judy understood the artist's challenges, the vagaries of success, and the stick-to-it-iveness that the arts demand.

I was hesitant to hire her. Here I was at a crossroads. My second novel had not sold and doubt was plaguing me: Was this idea to be a writer doomed? Misbegotten? Misguided?

Judy listened for a long time and then began to make recommendations. After about a year of working with her, I had still not placed my novel. "Establish yourself as a poet.

Your poetry is rock solid. Then you will have a base to go out to agents with for the book."

Her approach wouldn't have been my first choice, but I followed her advice.

I started winning prizes and publications. In three years, I had two poetry books accepted and won an international award for a chapbook of short stories.

After working with Judy for about four years, I had this dream. This essay was published in *Chicken Soup for the Soul: Dreams and Premonitions*. What my coach had taught me was that, even though I had always believed that the key to my happiness was love, it is really in work.

The Key

The first key dream was not what I wanted. Frank and I had been together for a few years, and I was sure that, after my divorce, Frank was "the one." He'd been a friend of my ex, Darrell, and had always been part of our small family.

I had a dream that Frank met me in People's Park—a popular Berkeley hangout spot with hippies and homeless people—to hand over the key to his apartment. I didn't take it.

A few years after that dream, Frank announced, out of the blue, that he had fallen in love with a woman at the office! I was devastated. In the six years that we had been together we had bought a new house in the Berkeley hills, had gotten married, and were living an enviably wonderful life with two blossoming careers. I'd had another child and was as happy as I had ever been—I thought.

Frank and I dismantled our lives, sold the house, and
separated our finances. I moved back to my old house that
I had rented out when we moved up into the hills. It was a
difficult transition, but the saving grace was that Frank was
more than happy to accept partial custody—he wanted to raise
the child we had had together with his new love.

Two years later, I had a dream that my ex—now back in the
picture as a sort of savior—handed me a key. I didn't accept
that one either. "It's too short," I told him. That dream helped
to settle the uncertainty I had been harboring that we should
get back together.

A couple of years passed as my daughter Simone, her
younger sister, and I rebuilt our lives. Simone was happy in
school; the baby was in full-time daycare, and my career as a
corporate space planner working with architects and designers
was taking off in wonderful and exciting directions. I was
promoted to Business Development Manager, overseeing key
company accounts. I was happy again.

I loved my children and my work and my funky, 1920s
Berkeley home, but still longed for a partner. Always
in a relationship, I now felt incomplete and lonely for
adult companionship.

Over the next two years on my own, I dated a string of
unappealing men who had no interest in my children. That
was a deal-breaker! I never even took the time to divulge that
"love me, love my children" was my line in the sand.

After numerous misbegotten dates, I berated myself for
wasting precious time. I dated men on the days when Frank
had the children—days when I should have been paying my

bills, fixing up my house, or anything other than wasting hours on disappointing men!

When Simone was eleven and the baby was four, I abandoned all hope of meeting anyone—at least while I was raising children. I came to a place of inner peace after a meeting with a financial planner. I was doing well financially, I was happy at work. I loved my life! I owned my own home, and had two wonderful children. I had friends and family. I would learn to live with what I had and stop wishing for what I didn't have.

Soon after the meeting with the financial planner, I met Adam. Adam was the man I had always dreamed of but had given up hope of ever meeting. A successful tech professional, he was divorced with two children close to Simone's age. He loved to read, he was an oenophile and gourmet cook, but, best of all, he loved my children! He was the most generous, loving man I could have ever conjured up.

The third key dream came after Adam and I were together for three years—right before we were married. In the dream, Adam was digging in the dirt, searching for a key.

Huh.

About a year later, I decided to change jobs. After eight years on the job, I had done everything I had set out to do. I was ready to commit to becoming a full-time writer. I had two degrees in creative writing, had published poems and articles in journals and papers, and was now ready to "go for it."

I hired Jane, a life coach who relied on her skills as a trainer, a therapist, and an intuitive. One day, after my second collection of poetry was published, Jane said: "Joan, I searched up and down Union Street for a gift for you. I looked at everything—

crystals, jewelry. Nothing resonated. Then my phone rang. I dropped it and when I got up, this key fell off the shelf."

"A key! Jane, you won't believe this!" I was shaking.

I told Jane the three key dreams. And, in that moment, I realized what the key dreams were telling me! A partner or lover, no matter how dear, cannot hold the key to me. The key is about my work; my real work of poetry and writing.

After that pivotal meeting with Jane, I was gifted with a fourth key dream. In that dream, I was hiding a key for Simone. I showed her best friend, Crystal, where the key was secretly hidden—on top of my rear car tire. "Make sure you tell Simone where the key is," I instructed Crystal.

I told Simone about the key dream. "For me, the key is about my work and my creative ambitions. I've hidden it away for you."

Even at twenty-four, I'm not sure that Simone really understood, but hopefully in time she will. Without the key dreams, I'm not sure I would ever have ever accepted that my life's true path, the key to me, if you will, is not about my partners or marriage, but about my work, my true passion, and about passing my wisdom down to my children, the next generation.

Social Anxiety, Shyness, and Social Media: Building Your Confidence

The Power of Social Media 101

Do enough readings, publish enough articles, stories and poems and reviews, and your Google search gets really interesting.

Add a radio or TV interview (you do NOT always need to have a book published to snag a radio or TV interview) by doing something newsworthy, and your name moves up in the search.

Having a name that is unusual makes you more "searchable," but what if there are 100 Katherine Browns or Wallace Smiths? If your name is Katherine Brown, how about distinguishing yourself with Katy T. Brown? Wallace Smith? W. A. Smith? Wally P. Smith?

Put that name on all of your business paraphernalia. With Gmail, you can even use your special searchable name for your email: katytbrown@gmail.com.

Meeting the Public

"Most people don't like public speaking," says Judith Horstman, journalist and professor. "It takes them out of their comfort zone." In fact, the fear of public speaking ranks in the top five fears.[8]

---

8   Christopher Ingraham. *The Washington Post*. "America's top fears: Public speaking, heights and bugs." October 30, 2014. https://www.washingtonpost.com/news/wonk/

If you are one of those writers who dread speaking, consider Toastmasters or other classes that help you to practice speaking in front of a group and speaking extemporaneously, thinking on your feet.

Social media can help the shy and the socially anxious reach and build an audience, but this writer still believes that the face-to-face meeting with your public builds your fan base in different, and important, ways. It's during the face-to-face that conversations like this are likely to ensue: "Oh, right, I was thinking about you the other day—I meant to introduce you to XYZ. I think he'd really like your work." Or, "I was telling my friend about your work. She said she wants to be on your mailing list."

Think of different ways to build your confidence, and don't forget that, by the time your book is published, winning writers have been building their fan base and working on their platform. They have a resume of publications and, ideally, they have been practicing, giving readings and interviews all along the way.

All of those public events help to build confidence.

Try an open mic, or ask to be a featured reader. You might find that you are more confident than you realize.

---

wp/2014/10/30/clowns-are-twice-as-scary-to-democrats-as-they-are-to-republi-cans/?noredirect=on.

Keeping Your Own Counsel Takes Confidence

I'm not sure why writers have such a hard time believing in their own work, but I have a sense that it has something to do with the process of invention.

After a number of rejections your confidence my start to flag. One reader tells you the piece is too long, one too short.

I have a dear friend who is a trained scientist. She is also an athlete who has always been interested in writing. Over the years she built up a fairly solid resume of travel articles and opinion pieces on public radio. The book she really wanted to write was about Vera Peters, a Canadian scientist who was the first to discover that radiology was a viable treatment option for breast cancer.

Peters' family allowed her to conduct research in the scientist's private archives. My friend invested in editors and made sure to have early readers. She had no shortage of opinions. She co-wrote an article for a scientific journal and had an excerpt of her book published in an anthology of writings about women innovators in the sciences.

When we had coffee, I asked where she was with the book. "I'm working on my memoir. I'm finished with that project." "Oh?" I pressed. "Why?" "One editor said it was too short for a book, and it's too long for an article. And, you know, some of it is about her husband, and family... I had two pieces of it published and that's that."

Did I mention that my friend had a connection at a Canadian press that was interested in the manuscript? Did I mention that this had been her obsession for over eight years?

"How many words do you have? Oh, and the part about the husband? That's great! This is a biography! Yes, your scientist lived a life of research and science, but she was a woman with a family, children. It's a great story."

"About 60,000."

"Dara! That's fabulous. Don't give it up!" I advised. "It's so tempting to move on to the next project. But you pretty much have a full manuscript. Have another editor take a look. See where you need to flesh it out. Before you know it, you'll have 80,000 words."

"Oh, I thought I needed 100,000 words, and I couldn't see where the other 40,000 were going to come from."

I told her that 60,000 words was certainly enough for a book. I encouraged her to keep her enthusiasm up about her memoir, but to keep pushing with the Peters book. She said, "Thank you so much. I know so much of my not wanting to keep going is the commitment. I heard a writer say that what writers really need is glue to keep them in the chair."

After our talk, my friend was buoyed. I could tell the book issue had been bothering her. She had gotten so close, and with the comments of a few readers, she had lost faith.

She said her issue was commitment, but I actually beg to differ. I think her reticence to go the distance with the full-length book was about a lack of confidence.

Dara is quite brilliant. But two life goals that were a stretch—running for public office and getting a PhD—were unattainable. She campaigned and lost. When she applied for a PhD in science, she was told that women should stay home with their children!

Being the author of a published book was the other big dream. Let me say that my friend has accomplished a lot in her life! She is an ultra-marathoner; she's ridden the death ride—a bike ride over five mountain passes in the Sierra Nevada. She's not a quitter. But, like most of us, she focuses on the activities where she is successful.

It's easy to brush off our lack of reaching our goals with, "Eh—whatever—it wasn't meant to be."

My hope is that you will take your project the distance. With the help of community, excellent craft, and commitment, you will succeed.

Tooting Your Own Horn: What Does It Sound Like?

Tooting your own horn can be as challenging as learning a woodwind instrument. Do you just pucker your lips and blow as hard as you can? Is that a sound your listeners want to hear? Or do you modulate your breath to create a mellifluous sound?

A winning writer who lectures on "Shameless Self-Promotion," Judith Horstman is a scientist who has seen the belly of the beast. A journalist, Fulbright scholar, and college professor, she is the author of five well-reviewed books on brain science.

When I interviewed Ms. Horstman for this chapter, she offered this advice for winning writers:

"When women promote themselves, they are labeled braggarts. When men self-promote, they are viewed as appropriately doing their jobs. Once, I was shamed by my own editor when I requested a speaking fee that was larger than what he thought I should ask for. 'You're shameless,' he said." Instead of fighting the derogatory remark, Ms. Horstman decided to 'own' the label.

Horstman continued: "Self-promotion, even when done properly, is often seen as 'not nice.' The problem is that in these times of diminished resources at the publishers, a plethora of books published yearly, and the constant 'noise' of media, the only one left to promote your work is you."

So where does this leave an author who, although she knows better, still cannot bear to promote her work?

"Focus on the product," Ms. Horstman recommends. "Do anything to distance yourself from your emotions. Pretend you are promoting someone else."

Also, she suggests, "focus on the 'product', i.e. your book, and not on yourself as the producer."

Another tactic Horstman recommends is to focus on your endorsements. "It's as if you are saying, 'hey, I'm not the one touting this book, look at what these experts say...' "

Ms. Horstman's books have been endorsed by media personalities and experts, including Dr. Oz, and by well-known medical professionals.

What the winning writer has to remember is that a writing career is all about numbers. The book that is published today will be analyzed by your next publisher. You have a chance of the strongest sales in the first six months of your book's life.

Your best strategy is to make a plan to get the sales numbers as strong as possible. Don't forget that that includes pre-marketing and hiring a good team to help. You've waiting a long time for this book; don't give up on it now!

Tools of the Trade

"Don't overlook the obvious," Ms. Horstman added. "Starting with business cards, references, clips of your work. Have a working, up-to-date website, social media profiles, a short bio, a long bio and a headshot at the ready."

Once again, a little research can go a long way. There are inexpensive ways to create business cards and great tools to create a website, too.

And don't forget about maintaining your website. New dates, info, publications should all be posted as soon as possible.

You Wrote It, Now Sell It

Part of building confidence and coming out strong with your new book is letting people know about your successes. We call that "tooting your own horn." It means that this is the time when the burden of publicity is going to fall on your shoulders.

The good news is that many people will be excited to hear about your book. The bad news is that tooting your own horn can occasionally backfire. (Read the story of Jane and Sarah below.) Either way, part of your job as the new entrepreneur is to toot your own horn.

Some people toot on Twitter, some on Facebook. Some stand up at readings and let their listeners know about their project and upcoming events. Some even run giveaways and contests.

Another way to let your fans know about your successes is with your monthly or bimonthly newsletter.

One job of the new entrepreneur is to stay visible. Your newsletter will keep you in front of that list you've been building the entire time you have been writing your book, and the groups in which you are active. You can post your newsletter to Facebook and Twitter as well.

Some toot their horns loudly; others toot theirs softly, or in a minor key. Some play the "Aw, shucks!" card. They show up for others, and keep the focus off of themselves. Fine! You can toot your horn by going to others' readings (this is advised in the Community chapter), you can toot it by reading at open mics (suggested in the Craft and Community chapters), you can do it online, and you can do it by going to meetings, showing up at organizations, and being known in the community.

If you are thinking, "I just want to stay home and write," I answer you: Of course you do! We all do.

A note of caution: Some authors toot their horns loudly, incessantly and, dare I say, obnoxiously!

Like the art of building community, tooting your horn is also an art.

Not too loudly, not too soft. Pleasant, helpful, inspiring! That's the major key you want!

I have three friends on Instagram who post pictures of themselves daily. Seriously? Do you think this inspires me, to see you eating food, drinking a cocktail, in a new outfit?

Think about what you are doing!

Creating Newsletters That Toot Your Horn!

Keep it professional, but now is your chance to get a little personal.

Why?

Because with a newsletter, people can leave anytime. But the ones who do want to get to know you can see a picture of you at an event, on a trip you took, etc.

Use your newsletter to build fans.

I got the idea to start a newsletter when I saw a friend's. If I hadn't seen her newsletter, I wouldn't have known that she was doing a writing retreat. What a great tool!

I thought a newsletter would be an efficient and fun way to stay in touch with my friends and fans. I would include new publications and upcoming events, and I also had a section on what my friends were up to, called "In the Community."

Boy, was I surprised when people told me how much they loved my newsletter.

I try to keep the newsletter light, informative, and fun. I'll use a quote from a favorite book, have pictures of friends, and always invite people to let me know what's going on in their world.

It's been a real success, a great and easy way to keep my name out and let people know what I am doing. It also helped me build my confidence.

I was writing something that people were responding to, and, as Judith Horstman recommended, I was doing shameless self-promotion, but keeping the focus shared with others, and not all about myself.

The Story of Jane and Sarah: How Tooting Their Horns Backfired

Jane and Sarah were two artists who met at a meditation. They soon discovered that they were both in transition. Jane had just quit her corporate job to write, and Sarah had just moved to California from Hawaii. She had left her graphics business and was struggling to build a small graphics firm.

The two took long walks on which they confided to each other about their dreams of succeeding in the arts.

After a few years, Sarah decided to go to work for a company. She learned web design. She seemed happy. Jane kept up with her writing, publishing three books in three years. She was quickly gaining a reputation as a winning writer.

She got involved with a national literary organization. With every new book, she did book tours, gave launch parties, and built her platform.

At a dinner party, she handed a new friend a postcard of upcoming events for a video she was launching.

Sarah was rude, and curt with her that night. It wasn't the first time that Sarah had commandeered the attention when Jane was talking about her work.

After some soul-searching, Jane confronted her friend of twelve years. "When we are alone, you are so sweet. Always asking about my work, so supportive. And we talk about your work too. But when we are with other people, you are so mean to me!"

Sounds childish, but it was true. Sarah owned it! "I don't like it when you talk about your accomplishments!"

Taken aback, Jane stood her ground: "I'm a writer. If I don't tell people, who will?"

"I guess I'm just jealous," Sarah admitted.

Jane was hurt. Why should her success diminish Sarah's?

Jane forgave Sarah and continued to support her in her quest to be known as a fine artist. She even gave her professional advice.

Three years later, Sarah was invited to show her work at a gallery. She thanked Jane for all that she had done to inspire and motivate her!

Moral: Just do what you do.

Don't worry about bruising others' egos.

Don't worry about what people think.

I call this keeping your own counsel. You have a dream that you are reaching toward. You might ruffle some feathers, but, along the way, you are making new friends, and fans.

You Are a Startup

"Fail fast."

—Steve Jobs

Get a group of writers together and the conversation inevitably turns to what, how much, and where. I am not talking about money. I am talking about book tours, talks, radio interviews, and public appearances.

Why?

Because these days, with a flood of books hitting the market every month, it is incumbent upon the authors to make the noise to get their books noticed. As we've said in previous chapters, getting your book noticed and sold is a critical component of being a winning writer. Your sales numbers will affect your future publications, and your writer's resume has an opportunity to glow with a new book out!

But this chapter is about confidence. How does acting like the founder of a startup, selling books, and becoming a winning writer intersect with confidence?

"Going into a room to network makes me want to vomit"

—Anonymous writer

The paradox of being a winning writer is that to be a great writer, your job description demands that you possess the ability to access the deep, gnarly, vulnerable, and tender side of your own, and others', psyches. The trick, the art, the skill, is balancing that most tender side of yourself—the side that has finally organized your life to shut the door, turn off the phone and write that book—with the most gregarious, confident, and self-assured self you can muster.

If this chapter is about confidence, what's up with: "You are a startup?" You're a writer, not a business executive. Right?

Well, half-right. I am a writer (as are you), but winning writers are also expected to embrace the "new entrepreneurialism."

Let me explain. In years past, an author delivered a manuscript. The publisher put marketing dollars and lots of muscle behind a book they had bought and believed in. Ads were placed in magazines and newspapers, sales reps talked up the book to bookstores, and, if the author was lucky, funds were available for a book tour to major markets and in the niche markets where the book would have a good chance of selling.

Their agent may also have set up a series of interviews, speaking tours.

Oh, that this was still the case!

The only authors who receive that sort of white-glove treatment now are major sellers. Dan Brown, John Grisham and the like. You get the picture.

Sadly, it is not you, especially with your first book.

Okay. But you still want to be a winning writer. So how do you meet the sales expectations of your new publishers?

You make your own plan. You hire a team.

You scour your lists and figure out where you know people. Who might invite you to read? Your local bookstore? Your alma mater? You make friends with your local librarians and book sellers.

You have spent time in the last year building up your fan base.

And, when launch day comes, you are prepared. Your press release has hit the market; you may have garnered a good review. Your publicist hopefully has set up an interview or a series of talks.

You still might arrive at an empty bookstore, come home with no book sales, or have to really push to get your book reviewed. Still, you are trying. You are a startup.

Startups are judged on how many users visit their site. If people are not jumping on board to download your app, and talking about it to friends, if you are not building your numbers monthly, then you are not going to be the one who gets the funding when the VC's (venture capitalists) hand it out. If that is the case, you're going to work pretty hard to get those numbers, right?

Same with the book.

You are the new entrepreneur.

The Story of Steve

Do you know how Apple started? Steve Jobs and Steve Wozniak, two "computer enthusiasts" (people, men primarily, who passionately played around with computers in clubs with engineers) got together. They were audacious! They rented a booth at tech conference and demonstrated a prototype. Yes, they had been testing this prototype and yes, they believed in it, but they had no company, no manufacturing, and no staff to handle orders. But take orders they did! They, as the urban legend has it, talked a good game! (Forgive me for using the example of tech, but my first career was in advertising. I worked on the Apple account at Chiat Day and was enchanted by Mr. Jobs.)

Take a page from their book and try it. When people ask you about your book, tell them about it with confidence!

What else does the founder of a startup do?

They manage their time. That means that they have a plan in place for the launch of their book, that they make time for events and for writing articles on their topics.

They work well with others (see "Meet the Team" in Chapter Four). They are the lightning rod for company enthusiasm. They are the cheerleader, the forecaster, the visionary, and the keeper of the dream. They are prepared for the reality that the publication road is not always smooth, even when that book contract is signed.

Many proactive "founders" believe that you should be doing at least one marketing activity every single day. That can include one nice note to a fellow author, activity on Twitter or Facebook or LinkedIn, taking out an ad for your book in a writer's journal, or placing flyers for your books in local libraries and in universities.

You can be giving talks at your writer's organizations, library, and even private salons. The importance of meeting the public in the first months that your book is out cannot be overstated. Are you heading out to visit your aunt in Des Moines? See if you can give a reading at a local bookstore. Don't forget: The farther you go, the more interested people are in meeting you.

A Note on Timeline and Spikes and Valleys

While your book launch is a critical moment, the story is not over in the first week, month, or even six months. Yes, you, and your team have been busy creating buzz around your book prior to publication and in the first months. But a glowing review can send your book soaring up the charts. So can a post-publication prize—and those are often not awarded until well after your book is out.

Like your search for your ambassador, you will be searching now for opportunities for sales. Can you speak at a writing salon, a literary festival? Can you do an internet radio show, an interview with a popular blogger? Is there a bookstore you never visited that you might be able to develop a relationship with now?

Starting Over

Sometimes, Confidence is Being Flexible Enough to Start Over

Teresa's great name change! Let's talk about how she started over.

Teresa Ryan changed her name and changed her luck. As she was looking to publish her first memoir, *Love Made of Heart*, Teresa was advised to add her mother's maiden name. She changed her name to Teresa Le Yung Ryan and sold her book. The way Teresa tells it, that name change changed her luck.

An acquiring editor I know is active in the writing community. She often attends conferences where authors pitch their book ideas to her.

But some authors are recalcitrant. When she, an experienced editor, advises a writer that his or her idea won't hold water in the marketplace, she often finds herself frustrated to meet that same author at another event pitching the same project.

Jobs' "failing fast" means being flexible enough to let go of a project if it is not working.

There is a thin line between having confidence in your project and being unable to see its flaws. Hopefully, that is a skill that you can access while you become a winning writer.

In the article, "The Home Front," by Lauren Collins in the January 1, 2018? issue of the *New Yorker*, Ms. Collins profiles Leila Slimani, the Goncourt-winning author of *The Perfect Nanny*. The Goncourt is France's highest literary prize.

Slimani was working as a journalist, covering the Arab Spring, when she decided to write a novel. "I knew that people were laughing behind my back, saying, 'Her husband earns a decent living. This story about writing, it's a polite way of saying that she's kept.' "

Slimani's first book is about a country that resembles Morocco during the Arab Spring—"It was really boring," she says. The dozens of publishers to whom she shopped the novel concurred.

She enrolled in a writing workshop where she met an editor who was also a publisher. He loved her work and published her first novel to great reviews.

By being able to say, "This is boring"—to let go of something she had devoted a year and a half to—she was able to move on to her next, prize-winning project.

Book Proposals

The Winning Writer's Book Proposal – Go For It!

The Essential Book Proposal

There's a common misconception that once your manuscript is finished, you write a lovely cover letter to an agent and pop it in the email. Done. Check.

Wrong.

When you write your letter to an agent inquiring whether they might be interested in your book, I recommend the following: place yourself in the agent's position.

Tell them that you are familiar with them and their work, that you have researched the authors they have published, and why your book might fit in well with their list.

Tell them about yourself. For example:

I am an award-winning writer, teacher, and editor living in San Francisco. I am seeking representation for [insert name of book], a novel of approximately three hundred pages that takes the reader inside the warp-speed world of a Silicon Valley gaming startup.

Give a short (two hundred words at most) synopsis of your book.

Tell them what other people have said about your book; your early readers and people who will give you endorsements, and tell them where your book fits into its genre.

The novel, which has been praised a "page turner" by early readers culled from the tech and literary communities, is thematically similar to Aaron Sorkin's The Social Network, Michael Crichton's Disclosure, and the recent film Margin Call. Also, similar to the characters in Douglas Coupland's Microserfs.

Tell the agent about your platform (in a condensed format) and about your accomplishments in the literary world:

I recently completed a term as President of the Women's National Book Association and am currently serving as

Development Chair. I have been a Huffington Post blogger since 2009 and am a member of the National Book Critics Circle, Poetry Editor for the "J," and Co-Poetry Liaison for the San Francisco Writer's Conference. I have also been a featured reviewer on Red Room Author's site. I have access to 15,000 Twitter followers and 3,000 Facebook connections.

Fiction

First, prepare a cover letter. In the cover letter, you introduce yourself, speak very briefly about your project (a paragraph), present your accomplishments, say why you wrote the piece, and provide a short sentence or two on marketing.

In addition, add these elements:

- A one- to two-page synopsis of your book (if it is fiction; nonfiction follows)

- A page of other books in your genre

- A page on audience: Who will buy this book? (Do you remember "platform"? Here it is!)

- A page on marketing: How will you market and sell your work

- A sample chapter or the first thirty pages

Nonfiction

- Cover letter

- Table of contents

- A brief pitch

- The first few chapters; one or two will do

- Your target audience

- Your marketing and platform information

- Other similar books in your niche

- Why you are qualified to discuss this topic

These proposals are not as easy as they appear. I labored over a book proposal for nearly five months! The trouble was that I changed the table of contents and rewrote my chapters, but the time was worth the investment. Regarding agents these days, remember I mentioned they'll ask about your platform. Well, before they can ask—you tell them!

Small Publishers Vs. "The Big Five"

Tinkers on NPR

When the Pulitzer Prizes were announced this past week, perhaps no one was more surprised than fiction winner Paul Harding. His novel, *Tinkers*, was released by a little-known publishing company with few works of fiction to its credit, the first time a book published by a small independent press has won the Pulitzer for fiction since 1981's *A Confederacy of Dunces*.

No one notified Paul Harding that he had won the Pulitzer. There was no congratulatory phone call. He wasn't sitting around with a group of friends waiting breathlessly for the news. Harding was alone when he checked the Pulitzer website, curious to find out who had won.

"I came as close to actually fainting as I think I ever have, because I literally just could not believe what I saw when it came up on the website," Harding says with a laugh. "And I kept refreshing and it just kept coming up *Tinkers, Tinkers, Tinkers.*"

Harding's short novel is the story of a dying man, George Washington Crosby, and his relationship with his father, who suffered from epilepsy and eventually abandoned his family because of the affliction.

After Harding finished writing the book, he sent it out to agents and publishers, but there were no takers.

"I just put in a drawer for three years I guess, and just thought this'll be one I have in the file cabinets and I'll just start working on the next thing," Harding says. "And then it was published more or less through a series of...wonderful, improbable accidents with the Bellevue Literary Press getting a hold of it and wanting to do it."

The Bellevue Literary Press was not exactly known as a powerhouse in the publishing world: The staff comprises editorial director Erika Goldman and an assistant. Their office is in a most unusual setting for a publishing company, "nestled," as Goldman puts it, "within the department of medicine at the New York University School of Medicine, which is at Bellevue Hospital."

Bellevue is a major center for emergency services in New York City, but it is probably best known in the public imagination as a mental hospital. The hospital's literary press was established five years ago, mainly for the publication of high-end medical books. But Goldman, a veteran of the publishing business, is also committed to releasing works of fiction with a scientific or medical theme. A publishing colleague who had passed on *Tinkers* because it didn't seem right for his company thought it might work for Bellevue.[9]

In NPR's Best Debut Fiction of 2009 list, John Freeman wrote:

> There are few perfect debut American novels. Walter Percy's *The Moviegoer* and Harper Lee's *To Kill a Mockingbird* come to mind. So does Marilynne Robinson's *Housekeeping*. To this list ought to be added Paul Harding's devastating first book, *Tinkers*, the story of a dying man drifting back in time to his hardscrabble New England childhood, growing up the son of his clockmaking father.
>
> The mystery and machinery of these ticking timepieces appear and reappear throughout this beautiful book, which cycles backward and forward in time, capturing with awful grace the unwinding of a life. George Washington Crosby, the book's dying hero, awakens out of delirium into the terror of his body's revolt. His loved ones, sitting nearby, might as well be in another country: that of the living, the healthy. Harding has written a masterpiece around the truism

---

9 Lynn Neary and Paul Harding. "For A Tiny Press, The Pulitzer Arrives Out Of Nowhere." NPR. April 17, 2010. Accessed May 21, 2018. https://www.npr.org/templates/story/story.php?storyId=126054322.

```
that all of us, even surrounded by family,
die alone.
```

Goldman says she responded immediately.

"It just leapt off the page," she says. "You know it when a manuscript arrives that is several cuts above the norm, and this was, this was it."

Goldman ordered a first printing of 3,500 copies, a small but not unusual number for a first novel from a small press. Then a sales rep in San Francisco fell in love with the book. She got the book buyer at the independent bookstore Book Passage interested, and that book buyer brought Harding to the store for a signing event. Soon he was visiting other bookstores and started getting invited to speak at book clubs.

"So, I went to people's houses and hung out with groups of eight to a dozen people and sat in people's living rooms and talked about the book and art and all sorts of pleasant things," Harding says.

The book, which had won glowing reviews from *The New Yorker* and the *Los Angeles Times*, started to benefit from a sort of ephemeral "word of mouth" buzz, Goldman says.

"This is a real phenomenon. It's not hyped. It's not heavily marketed and spun," Goldman says. "It's just passionate readers falling in love with a gorgeous work of literature and sharing the wealth."

Paul Harding drummed in the band Cold Water Flat. *Tinkers* is his first novel.

Eventually *Tinkers* had gotten enough attention in literary circles that the Pulitzer committee called Goldman and asked her to submit it for the award. But neither she nor Harding ever expected it to win.

About 15,000 copies have been published, and since the award, Bellevue has ordered another run, of 30,000. But even before winning the Pulitzer, Harding had gotten a contract for two new books, though not with Bellevue. His new publisher will be Random House; Goldman gave him her blessing. And the Pulitzer, he says, belongs to her and Bellevue as much as it does to him.

"When I step back a little bit," Harding says, "[I] just think this is just one of these really, really cool, wonderful literary anecdotes. But then what's mind-blowing to me is that I happen to be the protagonist."[10]

Working with Hybrid Publishers, Indie Presses, and Academic Presses

While all authors dream of snagging an agent to sell their book to a large publishing house, many writers place their first books with hybrid, indie, and academic presses.

Just be prepared to do all the heavy lifting.

---

10   Neary, Lynn, and Paul Harding. "For A Tiny Press, The Pulitzer Arrives Out Of No-where." NPR. April 17, 2010. Accessed May 08, 2018. https://www.npr.org/templates/story/story.php?storyId=126054322.

Hybrid publishers are ones who have an editorial board which carefully curates the manuscripts it will agree to publish. The author contributes to the production (printing, layout) of the book as well as taking on the marketing efforts.

Indie Presses are small presses—often micro presses—that are minimally funded. They will pay for the publication of the book, but often will not fund a publicity campaign or provide marketing support of any sort.

–Dos, Don'ts, & Challenges–

Do

- Listen to your dreams

- Listen to feedback, but keep your own counsel

- Celebrate every win! Every publication, every response with a positive note, every reading invitation, every completion of every project

- Get out of your comfort zone

- Toot your own horn!

Don't

- Second-guess the validity of your project

- Overemphasize others' opinions of your work

- Abandon projects that have potential

- Give up on your scheduled work plan

- Be afraid to scratch a project with no potential

Challenges

Do one thing that takes you out of your comfort zone every week, such as:

- Write to someone you want to know

- Go to a reading and talk to the author

- Send work to a journal out of your league or a contest you think you could never win

Resources

Online Submission Listings and Listservs

Creative Writing Opportunities—free to sign up. Will receive listings for submissions and teaching positions.

- New Pages
  https://www.newpages.com/

- Duotrope
  https://duotrope.com/

- Winning Writers
  https://winningwriters.com/

- The Review Review
  http://www.thereviewreview.net/

- Lit Lists
  http://litlists.blogspot.com/

- Poets and Writers
  https://www.pw.org/

- Submittable
  https://www.submittable.com/

Networking Groups

- PEN America
  https://pen.org/

- The Authors' Guild
  https://www.authorsguild.org/

- Women's National Book Association
  http://wnba-books.org/

- National Association of Memoir Writers
  http://namw.org/

- Association of Journalists and Authors
  (ASJA)
  https://asja.org/

- International Women Writers Guild
  https://www.iwwg.org

- Mystery Writers of America
  https://mysterywriters.org/

- Sisters in Crime
  http://www.sistersincrime.org/

- Romance Writers of America
  https://www.rwa.org/

- Books by Women
  http://booksbywomen.org/

- National Book Critics Circle
  http://www.bookcritics.org/

- Writer's Guild
  http://www.wga.org/

Online Classes

- She Writes University
  https://shewritesuniversity.com/

- Book Writing World Elizabeth Start
  http://bookwritingworld.com/

- Diane Frank
  http://www.dianefrank.com/

- Publishizer
  https://publishizer.com/

Many universities are offering online and low residency MFAs.

Literary Organizations to Join, Volunteer, and Connect

826 Valencia

826 Valencia is a non-profit organization in San Francisco, California, whose mission is to help children and young adults develop writing skills and to aid teachers in inspiring their students to write more effectively.

PEN

PEN is an international association of writers, founded in London in 1921 with the objective to promote friendship and intellectual cooperation among writers from all walks of life.

Reach Out and Read

A non-profit organization to promote literacy at the earliest stages of life and encourage reading within families.

Perry Klass

She is the National Medical Director of Reach Out and Read, a national literacy organization which works through doctors and nurses to promote parents reading aloud to young children.

The Author's Guild

A national professional organization for writers to protect their rights and interests, and promote free expression.

Publishizer

Publishizer is a crowdfunding platform that matches authors with publishers.

Writer's Relief

This organization helps writers' works find the right home with literary agents and editors to get published.

Recommended Books

- *Staying Sane in the Arts* by Eric Maisel
  https://www.amazon.com/Staying-Sane-Arts-Eric-
  Maisel/dp/0874776937

- *Poetry for Dummies* by The Poetry Center
  https://www.amazon.com/Poetry-Dummies-Center/
  dp/0764552724

- *Story Logic and the Craft of Fiction* by Catherine Brady
  https://www.amazon.com/Story-Logic-Craft-Fiction-
  Catherine/dp/0230580556

- *Burning Down the House* by Charles Baxter
  https://www.amazon.com/Burning-Down-House-
  Essays-Fiction/dp/1555975089

- *Walking Light: Essays on Writing* by Stephen Dunn
  https://www.amazon.com/Walking-Light-Stephen-
  Dunn/dp/1929918003

- *Story Genius* by Lisa Cron
  https://www.amazon.com/Story-Genius-Science-
  Outlining-Riveting/dp/1607748894

- *The Emotion Thesaurus: The Writer's Guide to
  Character Expression* by Angela Ackerman
  https://www.amazon.com/Emotion-Thesaurus-Writers-
  Character-Expression/dp/1475004958/ref=sr_1_1?s=bo
  oks&ie=UTF8&qid=1526672307&sr=1-1&keywords=the+
  emotion+thesaurus

- *Sin and Syntax: How to Craft Wicked Good Prose* by
  Constance Hale

https://www.amazon.com/Sin-Syntax-Craft-Wicked-Prose/dp/0385346891/ref=sr_1_1?ie=UTF8&qid=1526672383&sr=8-1&keywords=sin+and+syntax+constance+hale

- *Novel Voices* by Jennifer Levasseur
https://books.google.com/books/about/Novel_Voices.html?id=cponAQAAIAAJ

Books on Book Proposals

- *How to Write a Book Proposal* by Michael Larsen
http://a.co/bTPImU8

- *Shortest Distance Between You and a Published Book* by Susan Page
https://www.amazon.com/Shortest-Distance-Between-Published-Book/dp/0553061771

- *Bird by Bird* by Anne Lamott
https://www.amazon.com/Bird-Some-Instructions-Writing-Life/dp/0385480016/ref=sr_1_1?ie=UTF8&qid=1526673523&sr=8-1&keywords=bird+by+bird+anne+lamott

- *Chicken Soup for the Writer's Soul*
https://www.amazon.com/Chicken-Soup-Writers-Soul-Rekindle/dp/1558747699

- *You Are a Writer (So Start Acting Like One)* by Jeff Goins
https://www.amazon.com/You-Writer-Start-Acting-Like/dp/0990378500

- *How to Make a Living With Your Writing* by Joanna Penn
  https://www.amazon.com/How-Make-Living-Your-Writing-ebook/dp/B01081DQZ6

- *Master Lists for Writers* by Bryn Donovan
  https://www.amazon.com/MASTER-LISTS-WRITERS-Thesauruses-Character-ebook/dp/B016U2K20O

- *Self-Editing for Fiction Writers* by Renni Browne
  https://www.amazon.com/Self-Editing-Fiction-Writers-Second-Yourself/dp/0060545690

- *Writing After Retirement: Tips From Successful Retired Writer* by Carol Smallood, Christine Redman-Waldeyer, eds. Rowman & Littlefield Publishers (2014); 282 pages
  https://www.amazon.com/Writing-after-Retirement-Successful-Retired/dp/1442238305/ref=mt_paperback?_encoding=UTF8&me=

- *Reading Like a Writer* by Francine Prose
  https://www.amazon.com/Reading-Like-Writer-Guide-People/dp/0060777052

Magazine and Journals with Resources for Writers

- Poets & Writers
  https://www.pw.org/

- Writer's Digest
  http://www.writersdigest.com/

- Writer Magazine
  https://www.writermag.com/

- LitHub
  https://lithub.com/

Writer Services

Writer's Relief: This is a fee service. Writers apply for consideration. The service will help will various tasks—editing, manuscript preparation, and submissions.
http://writersrelief.com/

Publishizer: This is a service for writers that helps organize and strategize a pre-order campaign for a finished book. Research shows that Literary Agents and publishers are more apt to sign writers who have a book trailer, pre-orders, and a platform. There is a fee and an application process.
https://publishizer.com/

Reedsy: This is a self-publishing site for authors.
https://reedsy.com/

CreateSpace: owned by Amazon; a self-publishing site.
https://www.createspace.com/

Submit Write Now! This is a submission assistance service.
http://writersrelief.com/free-newsletter-for-writers/

The Write Life: One of the top 100 best websites for writers, including blogging, freelance advice and more.
https://thewritelife.com/

Scrivener: Software for crafting books.
https://en.wikipedia.org/wiki/Scrivener_(software)
https://www.literatureandlatte.com/scrivener/overview

How To Do It Frugally: This is Carolyn Howard-Johnson's website.
http://www.howtodoitfrugally.com/

Absolute Write
https://absolutewrite.com/

Other Sites/Organizations to Be Familiar With

Litcrawl: Does an annual weekly crawl that includes readings in Austin, Los Angeles, New York and San Francisco.
http://www.litquake.org/

Preditors and Editors
Alerts authors to unscrupulous editors, publishers, agents.
http://pred-ed.com/

Meet the Contributors

Andrea Alban is the author of nine books, including her debut YA novel *Anya's War* and *The Happiness Tree*. She founded the *Writer's Tribe* in 2012 at Book Passage and offers ReVision Retreats at her writer's studio in San Francisco. Visit her site for more information: www.andreaalban.com.

Tanya Egan Gibson is the author of *How to Buy a Love of Reading* (Dutton) and a freelance editor and writing consultant. Her articles about writing and editing have appeared in *Writer's Digest* and *The Writer*.

Mary-Rose Hayes is the author of nine novels, most recently *What She Had to Do,* including the *Time* and *Life* bestseller *Amethyst* and two political thrillers co-authored with Senator Barbara Boxer. Her books have been translated into sixteen languages.

Mary-Rose has taught creative writing workshops at the University of California, Berkeley; Arizona State University; the Squaw Valley Community of Writers at Lake Tahoe, and the San Miguel de Allende Writers' Conference in Mexico. For the past five years, she has been co-director of an annual writing workshop in Tuscany, Italy.

Ann Harleman is the author of two short story collections— *Happiness*, which won the Iowa Short Fiction Award, and *Thoreau's Laundry*—and two novels, *Bitter Lake* and *The Year She Disappeared*. Among her awards are Guggenheim and Rockefeller fellowships, three Rhode Island State Arts Council fellowships, the Berlin Prize in Literature, the PEN

Syndicated Fiction Award, the O. Henry Award, and a Rona Jaffe Writer's Award.

In an earlier life, having been the first woman to receive a PhD in linguistics from Princeton, Harleman lived and worked behind the Iron Curtain. Now, happily living within sight of San Francisco Bay, she is on the faculty of Brown University. She can be reached through her website, www.annharleman. com.

Kathleen McClung is the author of two poetry collections, *The Typists Play Monopoly* (2018) and *Almost the Rowboat* (2013). Her work appears widely in journals and anthologies including *Mezzo Cammin, Unsplendid, Naugatuck River Review, Peacock Journal, Postcard Poems and Prose, Raising Lilly Ledbetter: Women Poets Occupy the Workspace*, and elsewhere. Winner of the Rita Dove, Shirley McClure, and Maria W. Faust poetry prizes, she is a Pushcart and Best of the Net nominee. She teaches at Skyline College and The Writing Salon, and is associate director of the Soul-Making Keats literary competition. She lives in San Francisco. www. kathleenmcclung.com

Joyce Thompson is a lifetime storyteller, with six novels, two collections of short stories and memoir published. Her work has been translated into six languages and frequently optioned for film. She's taught writing at all levels, from Poets in the Schools to writers' conferences and MFA programs. After a couple of decades working as a technology product marketer, a job that uses and abuses writing skills, she's back to fiction and contemplating two nonfiction books.

Ann Gelder holds a PhD in comparative literature from the University of California, Berkeley and has experience as both a lecturer and program manager at Stanford University and as an educational software developer in Silicon Valley. An accomplished fiction writer, Ann has also published work in magazines and literary reviews. Her first novel, *Bigfoot and the Baby*, was published by Bona Fide Books in 2014.

Mary Mackey was born in Indianapolis, Indiana, and is related to Mark Twain through her father's family. While attending Harvard College, Mackey, an English major, came under the influence of the father of modern ethnobotany, Richard Evans Schultes, to whom she attributes a lifelong interest in botany and ecology, themes which often appear in her novels and poetry. During her twenties, she lived in field stations in then-remote jungles of Costa Rica. After receiving her PhD in Comparative Literature from the University of Michigan, she moved to California to become Professor of English and Writer-in-Residence at California State University, Sacramento (CSUS). She is married to Angus Wright, CSUS Emeritus Professor of Environmental Studies, with whom she frequently travels to Brazil.

Book club favorite and *New York Times* and *USA Today* bestseller **Meg Waite Clayto**n is the author of five novels, including the Langum Prize-honored *The Race for Paris*; *The Wednesday Sisters*, one of *Entertainment Weekly's* "25 Essential Best Friend Novels of All Time" (on a list with The Three Musketeers!); and *The Language of Light*, a finalist for the Bellwether Prize for Socially Engaged Fiction (now the PEN/Bellwether). I've written for the *Los Angeles Times, The New York Times, The Washington Post, San Francisco Chronicle, Runner's World*, and public radio, often on the subject of the particular challenges women face.

Stephen Kopel resides in San Francisco, CA; a blatant wordsmith of witty verse, he is the founder of the North American Butchers of the English language; author of *Spritz, Tender Absurdities, Picnic Poetry*; he invests in the "I Take Stock" market assets divided among kindness, rational thinking and good-looking humor.

Diane Frank is an award-winning poet and author of six books of poems, including *Swan Light, Entering the Word Temple*, and *The Winter Life of Shooting Stars*. Her friends describe her as a harem of seven women in one very small body. She lives in San Francisco, where she dances, plays cello, and creates her life as an art form. Diane teaches at San Francisco State University and Dominican University. She leads workshops for young writers as a Poet in the Schools and directs the Blue Light Press Online Poetry Workshop. She is also a documentary scriptwriter with expertise in Eastern and sacred art.

Joan Steinau Lester, EdD, the award-winning commentator, columnist, and author of four critically praised books, is also a freelance editor. A Bellwether Prize Finalist, Arts & Letters Creative Nonfiction Finalist, and NLGJA Seigenthaler Award winner, her writing has appeared in the *Alaska Quarterly Review, Essence, USA Today, LA Times, San Francisco Chronicle, Chicago Tribune, Cosmopolitan, NY Times Syndicate: New American Voices, Huffington Post*, Black Issues in Education, and Common Dreams. Her commentaries regularly air on National Public Radio's *All Things Considered*, San Francisco's KQED *Perspectives*, and Public Radio International's *Marketplace*.

She is the author of the acclaimed biography *Eleanor Holmes Norton: Fire in My Soul*, as well as *The Future of White Men and Other Diversity Dilemmas*, and *Taking Charge: Every Woman's Action Guide*. *Black, White, Other*: *In Search of Nina Armstrong*, her first novel, garnered starred reviews, and her second, *Mama's Child*, has just been released to critical acclaim.

Deborah Grossman is a sought-after San Francisco Bay Area journalist who specializes in stories about food, drink and travel. She writes for publications such as *Wine Enthusiast*, *iSanté*, *San Francisco Chronicle*, *Napa Valley Life*, *The National Culinary Review*, *Decanter*, *Wines and Vines*, *Flavor & The Menu*, and more.

Her recent wine and culinary travels include: Germany, Croatia, France, Spain, Chile, Australia, Italy, Mexico, Singapore, and Israel.

Deborah hails from Wilmington, Delaware. She worked for the DuPont Co. in Delaware, New Jersey, Mississippi, and Santa Clara, California. She began her journalism career by writing about food and drink in California and has broadened to a global gastronomic scope.

Peggy Townsend is an award-winning journalist whose stories have appeared in newspapers around the country. She's chased a serial killer through a graveyard at midnight and panhandled with street kids. In 2005, the USC Annenberg Institute for Justice and Journalism awarded her a Racial Justice Fellowship. Peggy is a runner, a downhill skier, and a mountain biker. She currently lives on the Central Coast of California. Follow her on Twitter @peggytownsend or on Facebook at www.facebook.com/peggytownsendbooks.

Andrena Zawinski is an award-winning poet and educator, born and raised in Pittsburgh, PA, who has made Alameda, CA, her home. She has authored several collections of poetry: Something About (Blue Light Press, San Francisco) received a PEN Oakland Josephine Miles Award. Traveling in Reflected Light (Pig Iron Press, Youngstown) was a Kenneth Patchen competition winner in poetry. Her chapbooks are *Taking the Road Where It Leads* (Poets Corner Press Honors Publication), Zawinski's Greatest Hits 1991–2001 (Pudding House Invitational Series), *Poems from a Teacher's Desk* and *Six Pack Poems to Go* Postcard Collection (Harris Publications). Her individual poems have appeared in *Quarterly West, Gulf Coast, Nimrod, Slipstream, Rattle, Many Mountains Moving, Pacific Review, Psychological Perspectives Journal of Jungian Thought, The Progressive Magazine* and others with several Pushcart Prize nominations and work widely anthologized. She founded the San Francisco Bay Area Women's Poetry Salon in and is editor of their anthology: Turning a Train of Thought Upside Down (Scarlet Tanager Press). Zawinski has been PoetryMagazine.com's Features Editor since 2000.

John Wayne Harold Foley was born August 9, 1940 in Neptune, New Jersey, raised in Port Chester, New York, and educated at Cornell University and the University of California at Berkeley. Foley's career as a poet is unique because it has always involved performance, specifically the presentation of "multivoiced" pieces written by Foley but performed by both Foley and his wife Adelle Foley (1940–2016). These pieces often feature conflicting, simultaneous voices whose interrelationships reflect Foley's often-stated belief that "some parts of the mind don't know what other parts are doing."

Foley met his wife, Adelle in November, 1960, while he was attending Cornell and she was attending Goucher College in Maryland. They married in December 1961; the couple had one child, Sean, born in 1974. The Foleys moved to California in 1963 so that he could attend UC Berkeley and she could work at the Federal Reserve Bank of San Francisco. Foley received an MA in English Literature at UC Berkeley and published several poems and articles, but by 1974, influenced by Charles Olson's *Maximus Poems*, he had dropped out of graduate school to pursue a career as a poet and writer. His first poetry reading, in which he read jointly with Adelle, was in June 1985. Since 1987, Foley has published has published fifteen books of poetry, five books of criticism, a book of stories, and a two-volume "chronoencyclopedia," *Visions & Affiliations: California Poetry 1940–2005*. His poetry books often feature accompanying CDs or cassette tapes on which Foley and his wife perform his work. Since 1988, Foley has also hosted a show of interviews and poetry presentations on Berkeley radio station KPFA.

Kelly Sullivan Walden, also known as Dr. Dream, is a dream expert, certified clinical hypnotherapist, founder of Dream-Life Coach Training, inspirational speaker, radio host, blogger, and author of seven books, including *I Had the Strangest Dream...*, a #1 Amazon bestseller in the Dream-Interpretation category. She is a regular commentator on Fox News and has done over 1,000 TV and radio interviews. She is also the founder of The Dream Project, an organization that inspires young people to access their dreaming minds to discover solutions to world issues. She has spoken by invitation at the United Nations and teaches with depth, playfulness, humor, and soulfulness to awaken people to live lucidly and creatively reveal the lives of their dreams.

Websites: www.DreamProjectUN.com, www.Doctor-Dream. com, and www.kellysullivanwalden.com

Jackie Berger was born in Los Angeles and received her BA in English from Goddard College in 1982. She studied under Olga Burmas and Jane Miller at Goddard, and later became interested in free writing and attended the Freehand Women's Writing Community in Massachusetts. Berger obtained her MFA from Mills College in 1995.

Since the late 1990s, she has been the Program Director for the Master of Arts in English at Notre Dame de Namur University (NDNU) in Belmont, California. Berger is also an assistant professor and director of the writing center at NDNU and teaches writing at City College of San Francisco. She draws inspiration from the dependent relationship between her teaching and writing career: "I really adore teaching, and it certainly inspires me. And I couldn't teach writing if I didn't write. So the two certainly work together."

In the mid-2000s, she participated in the Changing Lives Through Literature program, teaching prisoners at the San Mateo Women's Correctional Facility.

Karin Evans has been a writer and editor at many major national publications, including *Newsweek, Outside,* and *Health.* Her writing has also appeared in such places as *More Magazine*, the *Los Angeles Times* and *The New York Times.* Her book, *The Lost Daughters of China* (Tarcher, Penguin/ Putnam, 2000) was a national bestseller. With Amy Tan, she co-authored the text for *Mei-Mei: Portraits from a Chinese Orphanage* (Photographs by Richard Bowen, Chronicle Books, 2005).

Louise Nayer is a native New Yorker but has lived in San Francisco for over forty years. She attended the University of Wisconsin at Madison, and SUNY Buffalo for grad school, where she studied with poets Robert Creeley and John Logan. She received six California Arts Council grants and taught poetry in senior centers and nursing homes and was honored to hear so many amazing stories from older people. She taught many levels of English and creative writing at City College of San Francisco for over twenty-seven years and now she teaches small writing workshops.

She is a member of the San Francisco Writer's Grotto where she writes and also teaches. She also teaches at OLLI at UC Berkeley, and sometimes works with students developing their memoirs. She is working on her fifth book now.

She has two grown daughters and a step-daughter and lives with her husband and dog, Ella, in Glen Park.

Teresa LeYung-Ryan

Writing and platform-building Coach Teresa has helped over 1,000 writers. As a story consultant and coach, Teresa LeYung-Ryan identifies themes, universal archetypes, front-story, and back-story in clients' manuscripts. She is the author of *Build Your Writer's Platform & Fanbase In 22 Days: Attract Agents, Editors, Publishers, Readers, and Media Attention NOW*—the workbook for authors of fiction, narrative nonfiction, and prescriptive nonfiction (how-to books/ guides), for writers who want to be their own publishers or sell rights to other publishers. Teresa has built her own platform successfully and her first novel *Love Made of Heart* is used in college composition classes, recommended by the CA School Library Association, the CA Reading Association, and is archived at the San Francisco History Center. Coach Teresa's blog has abundant resources to help writes; visit for more information: http://writingcoachteresa.com.

Carol Smallwood's Women on Poetry: Tips on Writing, Revising, Publishing and Teaching is on Poets & Writers Magazine List of Best Books for Writers. Some of her over five dozen edited nonfiction books were published by American Library Association, Rowman & Littlefield, McFarland, and others. Carol wrote for the *Detroit News* and appears in: Who's Who in America; Who's Who in the World; Contemporary Authors New Revision (CANR) 282; Contemporary Authors Online Biography in Context; and *The Michigan Poet Collected Poems 2010–2015*. The multiple Pushcart nominee, a literary judge, reader, and columnist, has written dozens of reviews and interviews for such places as *New Pages, World Literature Today*, and *Rain Taxi Review of Books*.

Judith Horstman is a long-time journalist and author who has been a Washington correspondent, a university professor and a Fulbright scholar.

She specializes in writing about health, science and other complex issues in language we can all understand and enjoy.

Her lively prose is informative and fun to read. She's also a popular lecturer, workshop leader and interview subject.

Acknowledgements

Please note that two essays from this book appear in a slightly different form in *Women and Poetry: Writing, Revising, Editing and Teaching* by McFarland Press. One essay appeared in the *Book Baby* blog.

With that said, many thanks go to my assistant Daniella Granados, whose research enhanced many aspects of the book. Also, Renate Stendhal, my writing sister, inspiration and friend. Additional heartfelt thanks go out to:

To WNBA and my editor, Brenda Knight, and to Mango Publishing for believing in a holistic concept for becoming a winning writer.

To Wom-ba, Word of Mouth Bay Area, for stepping up with personal stories of struggle and triumph.

To my students who have inspired me with their drive, creativity, and motivation.

To my husband, Adam Hertz, my daughter, Simone Gelfand, and to David Wenk, who listened and helped me to fine-tune the ideas for *You Can Be a Winning Writer*.

To my writing friends and WNBA colleagues who sustain me: Mary Mackey, Stephen Kopel, Yvonne Campbell, Deborah Grossman, Kate Farrell, Jane Kinney Denning, Roz Reisner, Valerie Tomaselli, Carol Smallwood, Diane Frank, Rachelle Yousef, and Bebe Brechner.

To my coach, Judy Behr, who shows me the way, and to all of my publishers who have given me a step up: Gloria at Cervena Barva, Lois Requist at Benicia Literary Arts, Christopher Gortner and Linda Joy Myers of Two Bridges Press, and Robert Arthur of San Francisco Bay Press.

This book is dedicated to all the writers, whether in their dreams or in real life, whose books will join the literary canon, and to my ambassadors and beloved friends, Kelly Sullivan Walden and Dana Walden.

Joan Gelfand

The author of three acclaimed volumes of poetry, an award-winning chapbook of short fiction and a forthcoming novel set in a Silicon Valley startup, Joan is the recipient of numerous writing awards, commendations, nominations, and honors including PoetryMagazine.com's Poet of the Month, Red Room Writers, Poetica and The Noble (not Nobel) Prize from The Frugal Writer.

Her reviews, stories, and poetry have appeared in national and international literary journals and magazines including *Los Angeles Review of Books, Rattle, Prairie Schooner, Kalliope, The Meridian Anthology of Contemporary Poetry, the Toronto Review, Marsh Hawk Review, Levure Littéraire, and Chicken Soup for the Soul.*

"The Ferlinghetti School of Poetics," a poetry film based on Joan's poem, went viral on YouTube and was featured at the Fourth Annual Video Poetry Festival in Athens, Greece. The film won Certificate of Merit in a juried art show at the International Association for the Study of Dreams.

Joan coaches writers around the world by Skype, email, and in person.

For more information, visit her website joangelfand.com. For booking information, contact The Freelance Damsel: daniella.granados9@gmail.com.